BASIC SOCCER

BASIC SOCCER

Strategies for Successful Player and Program Development

George Ford

Head Coach, Men's Soccer
Harvard University

Allyn and Bacon, Inc.
Boston   London   Sydney   Toronto

Library of Congress Cataloging in Publication Data

Ford, George, 1937-
   Basic soccer.

   Includes index.
   1. Soccer—Coaching.   I. Title.
GV943.8.F66   796.334'07'7   81-10980
ISBN 0-205-07157-0   AACR2

Photographs by Barry Allen

The author thanks The Dexter School, Brookline, Massachusetts and St. George's School, Newport, Rhode Island.

Series Editor: Hiram G. Howard

Printed in the United States of America

Printing number and year (last digits):
10 9 8 7 6 5 4 3 2 1   86 85 84 83 82 81

*Dedicated to
my wife Susan
and
son Andrew*

ABOUT THE AUTHOR

George Ford has been playing and coaching soccer for nearly 20 years, and has held the position of Head Varsity Coach for Harvard University. Coach Ford was appointed to the United States Soccer Federation National Coaching Staff and Co-Director of the U.S.S.F. Eastern Regional Olympic training camp at The Pennsylvania State University and has directed various soccer camps throughout the country. He earned his B.S. degree from Rhode Island College and was awarded "A" certification from the United States Soccer Federation Coaching School at Rollins College, Florida.

CONTENTS

PREFACE

The purpose of this book is to provide coaches, athletic directors, and community recreation officers with guidelines for establishing and maintaining successful soccer programs. Methods of teaching game fundamentals and developing effective players are stressed. All aspects of America's fastest growing sport are covered.

In the late sixties, the collapse of both American professional soccer leagues appeared imminent. Phil Woosnam, North American Soccer League Commissioner, responded to the challenge. By focusing attention on the game's development at the grass roots level, he hoped to ensure the continual growth of soccer in the United States. Little did the commissioner realize that his message would be taken to heart by millions of people. Soccer has grown from an ignored, ridiculed sport, charged with being un-American, into a respectable national movement. Its popular appeal to people of all ages has been very exciting to those of us who have long been involved in promoting and coaching the game.

While the growth of soccer's popularity is encouraging, increased participation has created a serious shortage of coaches. Consequently, many potential young players lack the guidance necessary to develop their talents. In many cases, they are lost to the game. The call now is to "get involved." In my travels across the country, I have been told by numerous parents and young players that they would like to become involved. Unfortunately, few of these enthusiastic supporters have sufficient knowledge of the game to begin programs in their own communities. They ask: "How do I sell the game to sponsors and recreation departments? How do I organize and manage a team? Can I set up a sound and rewarding training program? Who will provide insurance coverage and medical attention in case of injuries?" Skill and technique are personal challenges to the player. Each player should devote much private time to perfecting them. Practice drills for skill and technique development will be covered extensively, along with the use of field markings, relay competition, and the grid system.

Modern-day soccer requires that all players be in motion at all times, with or without the ball. Players should be constantly looking for situations where movement will give their team a numerical advantage over their opponents. Ten tactical games are presented in Chapter 13. They will develop movement "on and off" the ball, also known as "reading the game." Individual, group, and team tactical maneuvers will be introduced.

Every sport poses a unique physical challenge. Soccer is one of the most physically demanding sports. Soccer requires anywhere from thirty to ninety minutes of continuous exertion; it demands endurance, speed, strength, and power. Fitness, therefore, is an essential part of any soccer program.

In Chapter 14, the coach is introduced to the three S's of soccer fitness: stamina, speed, and strength. Twenty exercises that improve strength will be explained. Both individual exercises and those utilizing the resistance of a partner are provided. The coach will become acquainted with sample games that improve speed and mobility. These games have the added advantage of varying training techniques.

Fun games stress working with the soccer ball. They allow the player to develop a "touch," or feel, for the ball, using all playable parts of the body. Ten fun games, along with the time and equipment necessary to play them, are presented in Chapter 15.

Suggestions regarding the selection, purchase, and care of equipment are offered in Chapter 16.

A glossary of soccer terms and references concludes the book.

ACKNOWLEDGMENTS

This book would not have been possible without the support, encouragement, and advice given me by the staff of the English and American coaching schools. Some coaches, however, deserve special credit. My special thanks go to Marc Charpentier, Carlos Pedro, Phil Pincince, John Kirby, Cam Pierel, Doug Tashijian, and Phil Wheelock. Over the years these coaches have tested, and are still testing, materials contained herein. They are recognized for their soccer expertise, and their enthusiastic, fun approach to coaching.

For inspiration, I thank Dettmar Cramar who established the coaching network in this country.

I would also like to acknowledge my assistant writer, Laird Boles of Dexter School for his patience and understanding in helping to change spoken English into written English. To Mike Smith for his section on the history of the game—thank you for a superb job. To my typists, Marion Gleason and Merrilee Torres, thanks for your time and cooperation. To all models, you look sharp.

LEGEND   FOR CHAPTERS 1-11 ONLY

CF_1 = CENTER FORWARD
CF_2 = SUPPORT CENTER FORWARD
RW = RIGHT WING
LW = LEFT WING
RM = RIGHT MIDFIELD
LM = LEFT MIDFIELD
SW = SWEEPER
CH = CENTER HALF
RB = RIGHT BACK
LB = LEFT BACK
G = GOAL-KEEPER
⊕ = SOCCER BALL
〰➤ = MOVEMENT OF PLAYERS
➝⊕➝ = PATH OF THE BALL
▷➝ = TEAM IN POSSESSION AND DIRECTION OF PLAY
●➝ = TEAM IN POSSESSION AND DIRECTION OF PLAY

CHAPTER ONE

Selling the Game

SOCCER: A BRIEF HISTORY OF THE GAME

Association football (better known in the United States as soccer) is, without a doubt, the world's most popular outdoor sport. The passion and frenzy surrounding the 1978 World Cup competition provide just one illustration of the game's universal appeal. Soccer is more than a game. In many societies, it is an integral part of culture, tradition, and legend. Soccer possesses an appeal so simple and natural that it will inevitably take its place in American sports culture as the game of the people, as it has in almost every other country in the world. Soccer, unlike baseball, is not an "invented" game, but one that has evolved over thousands of years.

Why study the history of soccer? First, it is a fascinating subject. Second, it is important for a serious player or coach to understand the game's background. The exact origin of the game is unclear. This can be attributed to the great age of the game and the many varieties of soccer that have existed throughout history. If we traveled far enough back in time, we might see prehistoric men playing a form of soccer, using the head of a slain enemy as the ball. Ancient Greek records describe a game called "Harpastum," played at athletic and dramatic festivals. A ball made from an ox's bladder was propelled by any means, fair or foul, across the opposing team's goal. A similar game was played by the Romans.

The spread of the Roman Empire took the game to Britain, where, even after the Romans left, it continued to flourish. Soccer in medieval England (known then as "football") was certainly a very different game from the one we play today. It was usually played on holidays between neighboring villages, with a goal set up in each village (these could be as

1

far as five miles apart). The game was simple and the rules virtually non-existent. The object of the game was to get the ball into the opponents' goal by any means short of murder. One observer of the time commented that: "Sometimes their necks are broken, sometimes their backs or legs, sometimes their noses gush with blood and sometimes their eyes start out."[1] Deaths were not uncommon. The violent and undisciplined nature of the game led King Edward III (and many subsequent monarchs) to ban football, imposing severe prison sentences on those who dared to participate. But the game refused to die. It was too firmly rooted in the tradition of the common man, and more than legislation would be needed to subdue it.

In the eighteenth century there was growing pressure to assign some rules to the game. This civilizing of football gained impetus from preparatory school and college headmasters who felt that a controlled form of the game would be a useful outlet for youthful aggression. When played at schools such as Eton, the game was really a mixture of soccer and rugby. As often as not, it was a chaotic melee. At that time there were no referees. If there were any disputes over foul plays: "The captains of the opposing teams would, in their manly, open way, settle all points of dispute."[2] (Imagine using that system today!)

Up to this date, football had evolved in a more or less haphazard fashion. In the nineteenth century, the game was to assume a new, definitive direction. On October 26, 1863, officials of several London football clubs met to form a national football association. The league grew over the next decade, but the game its members played was still a combination of soccer and rugby. Finally, in 1871, a group of Eton alumni formed the codified English Football Association. The EFA clearly distinguished between rugby football (played primarily with the hands) and association football, or soccer, in which handling of the ball in play was restricted to the goalkeeper. Rules governing team size, game duration, and the dimensions of the playing surface were very similar to the rules used today.

It wasn't long before the rules of the English Football Association spread throughout the world. Professional teams rapidly multiplied, national and international competitions grew in number and popularity. Soon soccer was being hailed as the "universal" sport. But it wasn't welcomed in the United States, except in a few colleges. A description in the 1827 *Harvard Register* recounts the annual struggle between freshmen and sophomores in a football game known as the "Battle of the Delta."

> The Freshmen's wrath, to Sophs the direful spring of skins unnumbered bruised, great goddess sing; Let fire and music in my song be mated, pure fire and music unsophisticated.

> The college clock struck twelve—that awful hour when Sophs met Fresh, power met opposing power; To brave the dangers of approaching fight, each army stood of literary might; with warlike ardor for a deathless fame impatient stood—until the football came - - -

'Let it be warned' a youthful Stentor cries 'No speeches here but let the football rise.' Through warlike crowds a devious way it wins, and shins meet advancing shins. 'Over the fence' from rank to rank resounds, across the rampart many hero bounds - -

. . .But ah, I vainly strive I could not tell what mighty heroes on the greensward fell, who lost, who won the honors of that day, or limped alas! Ungloriously away - - - -

The game would steadily become more and more civilized just as it had in England. By the 1860s, many colleges were playing soccer to some set of rules. However, team size varied from fifteen to fifty players, and the width of the goal might be eight or eighty yards. Even the scoring system varied from college to college. For example, in 1886 Rutgers beat Princeton six goals to four goals in which the victor was defined as the first team to score six.[3]

Widespread standardization came in 1907, with the formation of the American Intercollegiate Soccer League. This encouraged the establishment of larger leagues with common rules, and so brought about an increase in the game's popularity. By 1943, at least seventy-five colleges and many preparatory schools were playing soccer in well-organized leagues. A 1947 soccer handbook states: "Prospects for a banner year in 1947 are very bright—with soccer again revived on the Pacific Coast, being played in practically every New England and Middle-Atlantic college and gaining new footholds in the South and Mid-West."[4]

But such optimism was premature. Soccer did not rise to the level of popularity it was enjoying in Europe and South America. It was apparently doomed to lag behind American football, baseball, and basketball. Nevertheless, over the last ten years, due to factors such as media exposure, the emergence of world class soccer stars, and national coach's schools, we have witnessed a soccer "boom."

The most important factor behind the boom was the advent of American professional soccer in 1966. The National Professional Soccer League was made up largely of European and South American players, and teams such as the New York Generals, the Chicago Spurs, and the Detroit Cougars.[5] As a commercial venture, the pro soccer experiment was far from successful. Every NPSL team lost money. Yet, the venture marked a significant gain for the U.S. soccer. It brought soccer to the public's attention and showed how, even at the professional level, soccer was played by men of all physical builds (as opposed to the physical requirements of American football and basketball).

Today in the United States, soccer is beginning to filter down to the grass roots level. United States Soccer Federation membership has passed the half million mark, with 25,000 teams coast to coast. The message that soccer is every person's sport is finally ringing through to the public. There are few schools or colleges that do not include soccer as an important part of the athletic program. Indeed, there are indications that soccer is closing the popularity gap with American football. The professional leagues (NASL and ASL) are finally becoming financial and social successes. The young American player is inspired by the world class soccer stars now playing in the United States. Thus, more and more American-born players will enter the professional ranks. Within the next ten to fifteen years, soccer may become America's most popular sport. Indications are that America will, at last, become an influential member of soccer's universal family.

Historical facts of interest relating to U.S. soccer.

1840:	Soccer introduced at Harvard, Princeton, and Yale.
1862:	Soccer barred at Harvard and Yale because it is considered too rough.
1862:	First ten rules of the game originated by J. C. Thring.
1875:	Crossbar introduced.
1882:	International Board formed.
1884:	American Football Association formed.
1886:	First international game in North America played—U.S.A. vs. Canada.
1886:	First amateur game played in Central Park, New York City.
1890:	Kensington F.C. (St. Louis) first all American-born team formed.
1904:	Federation of International Football Associations formed in Paris.
1905:	First Intercollegiate Association League formed consisting of Columbia, Cornell, Harvard, Haverford, and Pennsylvania Universites.
1913:	United States of America Football Association instituted on April 5th.
1934:	World Cup competition in Italy took place with U.S. participation.
1950:	World Cup competition in Brazil highlighted by a major upset—U.S.A. 1, England 0.
1977:	Highest recorded paid attendance (77,691) to watch a soccer game in North America was reached when the New York Cosmos met the Ft. Lauderdale Strikers.

GATHERING MATERIAL

In order to generate program support, the coach must adequately prepare for meetings with local groups and recreational departments. Many questions will be asked about financing, injuries and insurance, field space, and number of participants. They must be answered correctly, with confidence and enthusiasm. The unprepared, uninformed coach is doomed to failure.

The United States Soccer Federation disseminates a great deal of relevant program information. The Federation is the only official governing body for soccer in the United States. It is recognized by the world governing body, the Federation of International Football Associations (FIFA). The Federation furnishes a multitude of services for the development of the coach's program—material on field procurement, insurance programs, financing, films, coaching schools, rules of the game, and a directory of certified coaches who may be called upon for assistance.

Another source of valuable information is the National Soccer Coaches Association of America. Membership is a must for the coach whose interest in soccer goes beyond the local team. The Association publishes a quarterly journal containing news on high school and college soccer, as well as articles written by well-known coaches. The association also holds an annual national convention for its members, offering three days of clinics, lectures, and exhibits by national and international equipment and aids distributors. Once the appropriate material has been collected, the coach should review and categorize it in order of importance for presentation to interested groups.

THE SELLING SEQUENCE

The Participants

The coach's first task is to stimulate the local youths' interest in soccer. In other words, the coach must sell soccer to the young people in the area. The coach should approach such groups as the scouts, youth clubs, and church fellowships. The leaders of such organizations are usually very receptive and they can guarantee an audience. When preparing to meet and present the program the coach must realize that a young audience will show little or no interest in long discussions about the game's facts and figures. An action-packed film or a soccer clinic that allows participation by the prospective players will be more effective. At the conclusion of the presentation, the coach should inform the audience that a team or league may be formed if enough young players are interested. At the same time, the coach should ask all those interested to register for the team.

The Recreational Director

The recreational director is the next individual to whom the coach must sell the program. This one person has access to all the necessary ingredients for promoting the coach's program. For example, the recreational director has a close working relationship with schools; access to all the schools' indoor and outdoor facilities; permission to post recreational programs and registration dates; fund-raising literature; names of businesses and organizations receptive to sponsoring teams; media support of recreational programs; and funding. It is very important that the coach make every effort to win this person over.

The coach must take advantage of whatever resources are offered. In the beginning, the coach may receive a minimum of assistance, third-rate fields, and restricted financial help. After all, the main function of the recreation department is to meet the needs of all supervised youth programs. Most recreation departments are scheduled around more established sports, such as baseball and football. As the soccer program gains recognition, conditions will improve.

The Athletic Director

The coach wishing to introduce an inter-scholastic league to the schools should not approach the athletic director until he or she has evidence of student interest and support. A sound recreational program will substantially contribute to student interest. The athletic director must then be presented with the potential number of participants, estimated cost, and evidence of a trend toward inter-scholastic soccer competition.

Sponsors

Once the coach has the required number of players and the support of the recreational director, soliciting sponsors to finance equipment is the next priority. The coach should contact local groups, such as the Lions, Rotary, and Kiwanis for permission to present the program. Present a short, action-packed soccer film, and briefly outline the program. Emphasize the popularity of soccer, its minimal cost, its widespread appeal to young people—you don't have to be very tall, or very muscular, to play soccer. Appeal for sponsors at the conclusion of the meeting, and ask interested parties to get in touch as soon as possible. The coach's success in soliciting sponsors will depend on the presentation's effectiveness. Convince the audience that participating in the program will provide wide advertising exposure of their organization or product at a nominal cost.

MEDIA SUPPORT

The coach can take advantage of free press, radio, and television advertising by planning a clinic featuring professional players or college coaches or a talk show centered around a professional player or coach.

The talk show host might emphasize soccer on all levels and plug the local program. Since soccer is now socially accepted and newsworthy, the media are as anxious as the coach to establish a working relationship.

REFERENCES

1. Brian Glanville, *Soccer* (New York: Crown, 1968), pp. 3–4.
2. Ibid., p. 12.
3. U.S. Department of the Navy, Aviation Training Division, *Soccer* (Annapolis: United States Naval Institute, 1943), p. 5.
4. *NCAA Official Soccer Guide 1947* (New York: A. S. Barnes, 1947), p. 15.
5. Glanville, *Soccer*, Chapter 10.

CHAPTER TWO

Team Management and Organization

PERSONALITY AND QUALITIES OF THE COACH

Experience

The coach's greatest worry is often his or her lack of teaching or playing experience. Although experience is a powerful tool and a prerequisite for advancement, for a coach of young novices it is not nearly as important as the coach's personality. Personality will determine the coach's success, whether the desired outcome is a "fun game" free of physical and mental pressures, or the building of a powerful, homogeneous team.

Knowledge of the Game

Knowledge of the game's rules, strategies, and tactics is a basic requirement for obtaining player respect. It is important that the coach make every effort to become a student of the game, reading many of the excellent available books, attending soccer clinics and schools, and observing games at all levels.

Enthusiasm and Interest

During a training program, the coach must assume the role of a salesperson. The coach must be dynamic and persuasive, and believe in this product that has stirred the interest of countless people across the country. Once interest has been developed, the coach's job of motivating players will be a relatively simple task, if training regenerates interest. It is also important that the coach be very receptive to players' needs and input regarding program objectives. A short question and answer period before and after each session will ensure that interest in the program is maintained.

Ability to Demonstrate

The ability to demonstrate is not a prerequisite of good coaching. The coach who has this attribute, however, may have more confidence. If a coach is unable to demonstrate, it will be necessary to seek assistance from state coaches, local professional players, college players, and training films.

Ability to Elicit Quality Performance

A good coach demands quality. The coach must constantly strive to elicit an impressive performance from his or her players. Successful and attractive soccer depends on fighting spirit, physical fitness, and being in top form at the right moment!

Persistence and Patience

A coach who ignores or cannot recognize a player's inability to perform a task is asking for trouble. Setting impossible goals frustrates the novice player. The player's desire to learn diminishes when he or she cannot perform. Skill development is built on player motivation, and must be patiently built up from practice session to practice session.

Ability to Keep to Priorities

The coach must plan a step-by-step method of learning that meets the needs of all the players. Players must be guided through each new experience, and have sufficient opportunity to put previous lessons into practice. Only when each player understands and has mastered a skill should a new lesson be introduced.

Singlemindedness

The coach should be genuinely interested in the players' physical skills and their social and moral conduct. Sportsmanship, team play, and positive attitudes must be stressed. All can help further develop the players' performance. The coach should also be honest with the players and sensitive to individual needs and anxieties. The coach who is dedicated to fulfilling these requirements will be rewarded when players demonstrate their expertise in total soccer. Strength of character in defeat as well as in victory will brighten the players' ensuing years.

Empathy with the Learning Process

Understanding the learning process will help the coach achieve solid player and team development. The first step in understanding how the individual learns new skills is to determine the roles assigned to the coach and the player. The coach must inspire the player to learn through motivation, player involvement, demonstration, and guidance. To learn, the player must actively participate in an exercise designed to change the player's way of thinking and acting. The player must do something that will make the mind and muscles behave differently. Not only must the player receive new skills from the coach by observing and listening; the player must also be encouraged to use these skills and ideas at every opportunity. Only when the player is able to utilize what has been shown, heard, or read is the learning process complete. In other words, telling is not coaching, listening is not learning, and watching is not learning; but all three are tools of learning. Learning requires active experience.

Imagination

Stimulating and motivating players makes practices enjoyable and rewarding. The coach must try to create situations that challenge the players' imaginations, appeal to their pride in personal performance, and serve as meaningful game drills.

Several examples of motivational stimuli that have met with success are offered in this book. However, it is essential that the coach adopt the style that best suits his or her personality. Coaches choosing to use the methods given here should do so only until their own unique techniques elicit greater response.

SETTING UP THE PROGRAM

Meeting the Players

A team may be formed in one of four ways. First an established league may have a draft and tryouts, during which the coach selects players. Second, the coach may volunteer or be assigned to an organized team. Third, the coach may receive a list of players who have registered from a certain geographical region. Fourth, the coach may have to hustle players from the streets, playgrounds or schools if a new team or league is to be formed.

Once the coach has the required number of players, they should be informed of the time and location of the first official practice session. Each should be encouraged to furnish his or her own soccer ball.

Gearing the Session

The coach should gear the training sessions to the age group of the players. It is important that the coach know the age group's physical and mental characteristics; adapt the training program to suit the players; and set the level of competition according to the stage of physical and mental development of the players.

For example, suppose one has a group of youths, ages ten to twelve. In comparison to those of the eight-to-ten age group, physical characteristics at this level are a longer period of endurance, due to increased heart and lung size; increased muscle strength; and improved coordination and reaction time.

Mental characteristics at this level are longer attention span; increased intellectual curiosity; more emotional control in individual and group situations; greater independence and peer group identity. Players in this age group understand the concept of team performance; enjoy competition; are tough, fearless, and energetic. The coach, therefore, must offer competitive team games encompassing the players' basic skills and tactical awareness. The coach can also give the players tasks that demand more power, endurance, speed, and ability.

THEY HAVE COME TO PLAY

There is a natural tendency among coaches to overorganize and expect too much from young players. Emphasis on systems of play, regimentation, and restricted player movement is unfortunately, still a large part of the American soccer scene. One can sympathize with these methods when one realizes that many coaches are hustled into a soccer program, given a ball and a squad of novice players, and told that they have a game in one week.

A coach must keep in mind that his or her recruits have come to play soccer, the world's most popular and exciting game, because it is one of the few remaining team sports that encourages freedom of thought and movement. The current free-wheeling brand of soccer has set new challenges for both coaches and players.

The shackles placed upon players prior to the early 1950s, which somewhat restricted their freedom of movement, are hopefully gone forever.

The coach must know the strengths and weaknesses of each player before establishing a set system of play. Setting positions beforehand will produce a mechanical, unimaginative team. All too often one hears comments from young players such as, "I am a forward and so my job is to score goals," or "I play in the defense and I help to stop the other team from scoring." Pity the poor midfielder, who, when asked what his function is, may reply, "I am not sure, but I do take the throw-ins." *They have come to play*, period. They have come to run, kick, and dribble the ball. Of course, a player must be assigned a position as a base of operation. But once the game is in progress, stressing positions, systems of play, and restricted movement will only dampen the spirits of all concerned.

At the first practice session, the coach should have them immediately begin play. At the outset, setting up soccer games with five or six players on each side, as opposed to a full-sided eleven versus eleven game, will provide better enjoyment and foster skill development. With fewer players participating in the games, player deficiencies are more readily recognized, recorded, and corrected. The small-sided games, whether five versus five or one versus one, are the basis from which future player, team, and coaching success will be realized. The purpose of the soccer program should be to offer the young players the best possible outlet for their energies. The small-sided game reflects qualities that are essential to a high level of player interest, growth, and skill development.

PLAYER APPRAISAL

The strength and success of a team depends upon each player's ability. Every new coach dreams of having the ideal team. All the players on this team are total soccer players. The only thing the coach has to do is mold these perfect players into a viable unit.

The total soccer player should have the physical qualities of speed, strength, and stamina, plus an impressive array of psychological qualities. The total player is competitive, determined, courageous, aggressive, and competent "on" and "off" the ball. This player has tactical understanding, knows the game, and is easy to coach. Of course, one very rarely finds these qualities in the young novice player. However, some basic traits will be evident. The ability to adjust to a team's strengths and weaknesses is a prerequisite to coaching success.

One of the quickest and most reliable methods of judging players is through the extensive use of small-sided games. Players' physical and psychological characteristics will stand out when fewer participate in a restricted area. The coach must weigh various factors when forming the team. Does any one player demonstrate outstanding leadership ability to which other players respond? If so, this player can be invaluable in player–coach relations and team motivation. Do certain players show great fighting spirit, aggressiveness, and determination to win possession of the ball? Are some players more coordinated than others, can they move laterally, turn, jump, and run with ease? Are some players confident and competent handling the ball? Or do they quickly pass it, without regard for a supporting player's situation? Do certain players adopt attacking and defending roles with a sense of responsibility, confidence, and poise under an opponent's pressure? Are some players more mentally alert than others? Do they see and create situations that could lead to, or prevent, goals being scored? What are the players' reactions to winning or losing the game, or an individual battle? What are the players' feelings toward the game in general? Briefly, these are some of the basic considerations that influence the coach's decision-making process. Only after answering these questions can the coach assign player positions and form the team.

ASSIGNING POSITIONS

Decisions on how to utilize talent and how to form the starting team will have to be very tentative at first. (See Figure 2–1.) In the first few games, formation should serve only to give the players self-identity and

Figure 2–1. Team formation 4–2–4 base of operation.

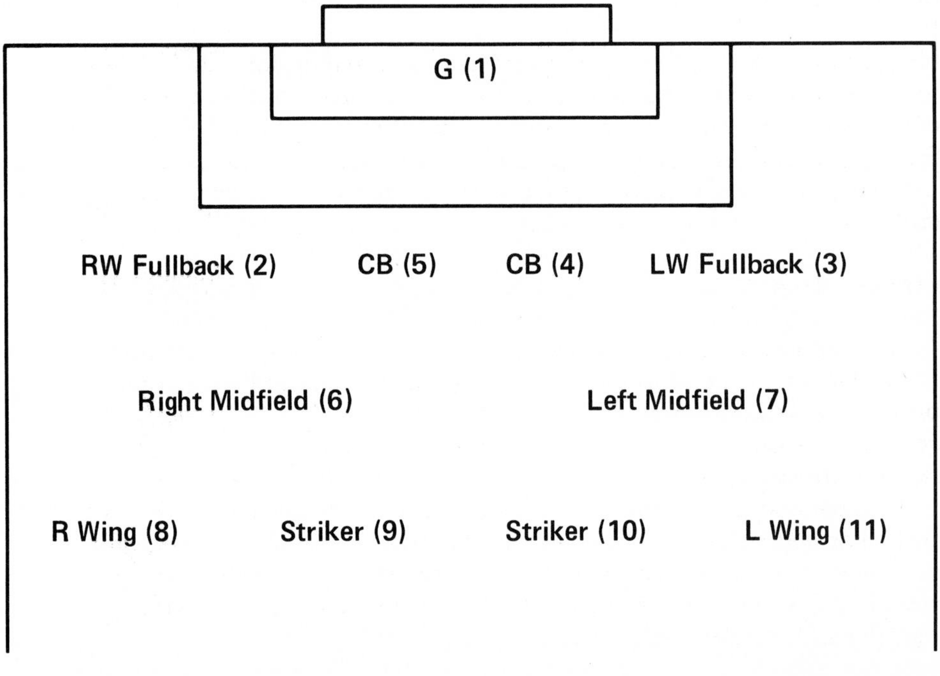

a place to stand at the start and restart (when goals have been scored) of the game. Players must have the opportunity to try other positions during the course of the season and be assigned certain minor responsibilities, such as "throw-ins" and "free kicks," to foster confidence. Team formation should be flexible enough to adjust to the players' development in skill, positional sense, and basic knowledge of the principles of play.

The Goalkeeper

It is a myth that the larger the goalkeeper, the less likelihood there is of goals being scored against the team. The goalkeeper, in fact, should be the epitome of coordination, possessing the agility and poise of a gymnast, the hands and timing of a wide receiver, the courage of a hockey goalie. The coach must be very careful when assigning a young player to this very demanding position, and must make a selection only after a number of workouts have shown that a player has the necessary qualities. (See also chapters ten and eleven.) At the outset the coach should assign players with the desired physical and psychological traits to defensive positions, until the strength of competing teams can be tested.

Wing Fullbacks

The modern-day wing fullback must be able to adopt both defending and attacking roles as the flow of the game dictates. When assigning young or novice players to these positions, the coach must clearly state that their first and most important task is to defend their own goal. The responsibilities of the wing fullback are: to man mark or close down very quickly the opposing winger whenever the ball is in the general area; to support other defending players; and, most important of all, to be a ball winner. Strength, speed, concentration, aggressiveness, decisiveness, and a basic understanding of the principles of defense make a good wing fullback. (See chapter three.)

Sweeper Back

The sweeper back is basically a "free man" sweeping or moving, from touchline to touchline behind a four-person defensive line. The deployment of a sweeper is primarily an extra defensive measure. The sweeper's responsibility is to cut off any penetrating runs or passes through the four defenders. Since this is a highly specialized position, the coach must assign it to the player who shows a natural talent for defending and being in the right spot at the right moment. The satisfactory sweeper back will have speed, strength, stamina, awareness, decisiveness, confidence, and poise. The player should also have a basic understanding of the principles of defense.

Center Halfback

The center halfback is commonly referred to in most soccer playing countries as the "king pin" or "keystone" of the team, because of the player's commanding influence and physical attributes. The center halfback is mainly a central defender, responsible for thwarting attacks through the center of the field and the penalty-area by making timely tackles and interceptions. A ball winner, the center halfback is always within range of the opposing team's lead striker. The player assigned to this position must possess outstanding physical qualities, such as height, speed, strength, and stamina. The center halfback's psychological arsenal must be second to none, and include tenacity, assertiveness, decisiveness, confidence, and self-discipline. The player should also have a basic understanding of the principles of defense.

Midfielders

Midfielders are called the "spark plugs" or "play makers" of the team. The midfielders' prime function is to set the team's pace. They will ignite the team to a frenzy or slow it down to run smoothly. In tune with each other, they slow down or speed up the pace in accordance with game conditions. Midfielders out of tune with each other or bypassed by supporting players can make the team sluggish, disorganized, and ineffective. Required to work very hard both in attack and defense, the midfielder must display outstanding fitness and an appetite for possession of the ball. When assigning young or inexperienced players to these positions, the coach must select players who display a noticeably high work rate. Stamina, strength, speed, competitive fighting spirit, determination, and confidence on and off the ball are prerequisites, along with a basic understanding of the principles of attack and defense.

Wingers

Many adjectives (maestro, ghost, bird, clown) have been used to describe the almost magical and fleeting attributes of the winger. The winger is primarily an offensive player who either attacks or stays wide along the flanks to keep the opposing defense stretched. The modern day winger is also expected to support in defense. More often than not the winger is the smallest, leanest, and least physical member of the team, relying on exceptional dribbling skills and guile to avoid and beat an opponent. When assigning a young novice player to this position, the coach should consider one who lacks height and strength, but possesses speed coupled with some natural dribbling skills. Psychological qualities demanded of this position are confidence on the ball, courage to take on players who are sometimes bigger and more aggressive, and a basic understanding of the principle of width in attack.

Strikers

Called the "hot shots" of the team, strikers are the main thrust of the attack, accumulating the lion's share of goals scored during the course of a season. Working closely together, sharing the responsibilities of feeder and lead striker, these players are continually adjusting their positions to seek passes deep in their opponent's defense. When assigning these positions to young players, the coach must select those who demonstrate a flair for scoring goals and not much inclination toward defensive responsibilities. The physical characteristics needed for these positions are speed and strength. Since these players often receive the ball with their backs toward their opponent's goal, they become targets for powerful challenges from behind. Thus, strikers must be totally aware of their position in relationship to the opponent's position, courageous, determined to pursue the ball, able to take considerable punishment, and confident of victory.

HOW TO USE PARENTS AND PLAYERS IN ADMINISTRATIVE POSITIONS

Effective use of parents and players in supporting roles is vital to the team's existence and efficiency. The coach should take full advantage of these valuable resources by delegating responsibilities that might otherwise restrict the coach's effectiveness.

Players in supporting roles:

1. Assist in the placement and the removal of goal, nets, cornerflags, etc.
2. Assist in marking the field of play.

Parents in supporting roles (on a rotating basis):

1. Assist the coach at the practice session in a supervisory capacity.
2. Assist in the transporting of players to and from games and practices.
3. Are responsible for refreshments.
4. Organize and carry out fund-raising projects to ensure the team's financial stability.
5. Attend periodic coach-parent social meetings to maintain team unity.

CHAPTER THREE

Fundamental Principles of Play

Although systems and coaching methods have changed, the principles of play (Figure 3–1) have remained intact. They are still emphasized in all national coaching schools throughout the world.

Modern-day soccer demands that all players be able to adapt to both attack and defense roles, with a minimum of team disruption. Thus, the coach and each member of the team must understand that at the moment ball possession is lost, *all players become defenders* and abide by the principles

Figure 3–1.

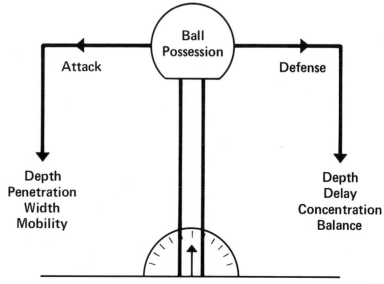

of defense. Similarly, the moment ball possession is regained, *all players become attackers* and abide by the principles of attack. Goal scoring and goal stopping are everyone's business.

BALL POSSESSION

In soccer, the most important principle is ball possession. Until the ball is lost, the ball-possessing team will dictate play and minimize scoring threats on its own goal—two critical functions.

Soccer is like a jigsaw puzzle. All aspects of the game must be pieced together to complete the picture. In order to maintain ball possession, players must be well trained in individual skills, and understand the principles of play, and be both physically and mentally fit.

Of course, mere ball possession does not ensure a victory. A team may have possession of the ball most of the time and still lose the match. However, the more often you possess the ball, the greater your chances are of winning a game.

DEPTH IN ATTACK

Depth in attack depends upon ball possession and a team's effort to maintain possession. Supporting players must be within passing range of the ball carrier to maintain depth in attack. Ideally, supporting players should be able to composedly receive, control, and pass the ball.

In Figure 3–2, RM has possession of the ball and is well supported in depth by players RB, LM, RW, CF_1 and CF_2. This allows ball carrier RM a full range of passing opportunities. It is important to note that no two supporting players are lined up with each other and the ball carrier. The ideal field position consists of a series of interlocking triangles, with at least three players supporting the ball carrier.

Many attacks break down because forward players get caught standing or running in a straight line toward their opponent's goal. Should the ball reach them, defending players can immediately apply pressure by making timely tackles and interceptions or using the off-sides trap. Attacks may also fail because forward players charge like Custer's Seventh Cavalry toward their opponents' goal and away from the ball carrier. The ball carrier must powerfully kick the ball over or through the opposing defense, so that the forward players can catch up with and control the ball. But the forward players seldom reach the ball in time. Because of its speed the ball either is gathered in by the goalkeeper or runs over the goal line and out of play for a goal kick.

In Figure 3–3, RM has ball possession but no depth in attack. Players

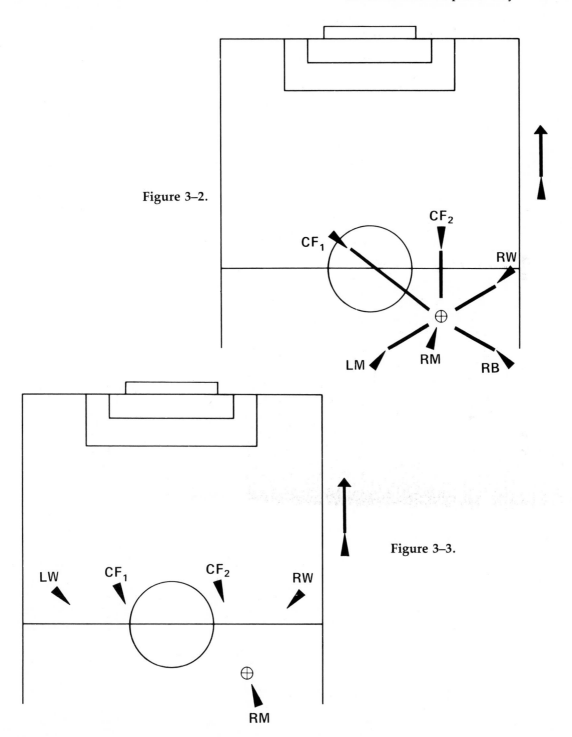

Figure 3–2.

Figure 3–3.

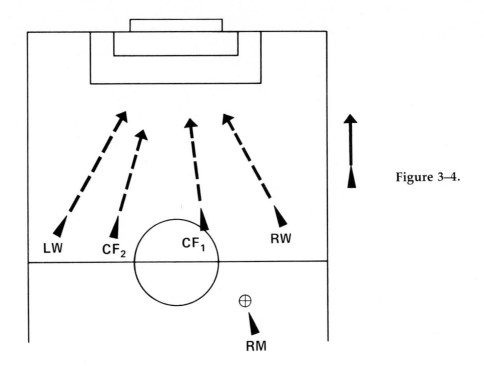

Figure 3–4.

RW, CF_1, CF_2, and LW are standing flat and are reducing the range of passing opportunities to a back pass only. The threat of off-sides and interceptions by the defending players must also be considered by player RM.

In Figure 3–4, RM has possession of the ball, only to see forward players RW, CF_1, CF_2 and LW sprinting down the field and reducing the range of passing opportunities. Undue pressure has been placed upon RM. Now RM must decide whether to maintain possession of the ball and hope for support, or to make a fifty-yard pass that will be up for grabs.

DEPTH IN DEFENSE

Depth in defense is just as critical as depth in attack. The defending side must at all times try to avoid being caught flat, especially in their own territory. Ideally, a player will make a challenge for the ball to slow down the play and turn the ball carrier toward the touchline. At the same time, supporting players will move into central covering positions.

In Figure 3–5, the three defending players RB, CH, and LB are caught flat. Should ball carrier LW decide to penetrate the space between RB and CH, either by dribbling or by setting up a wall pass situation with sup-

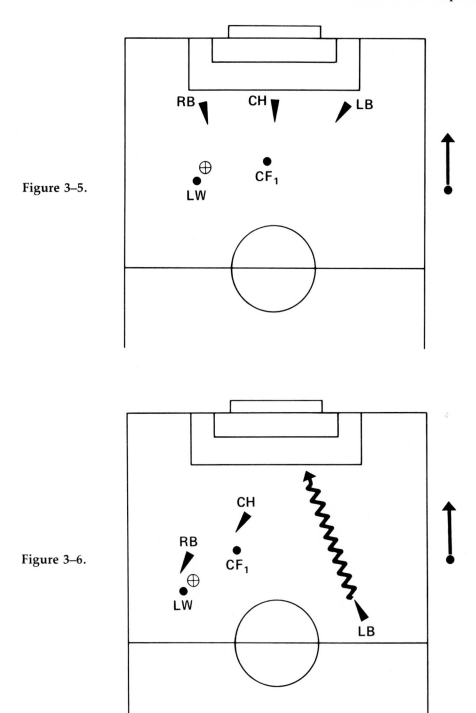

Figure 3–5.

Figure 3–6.

porting player CF_1, all three defending players LB, CH, and RB would be played out of the game.

By contrast, in Figure 3–6, there is depth in defense and support for challenger RB. Supporting defensive player CH is in position to make an immediate challenge for the ball should LW decide to pass the ball to CF_1 or attempt to dribble past RB. Meanwhile, supporting defensive player LB races back to support player CH.

Failure to support the defensive player making the initial challenge can create problems that result in goals.

PENETRATION IN ATTACK

Utilizing penetration in attack means creating situations that allow the ball carrier or supporting players to dribble the ball through space or receive the ball in space. These moves can be devastating. They can eliminate from two to ten defending players, depending on where the run or pass initiated. Sizing up the situation and moving the ball quickly are essential.

In Figure 3–7, RM is in possession of the ball and passes to RW. RW

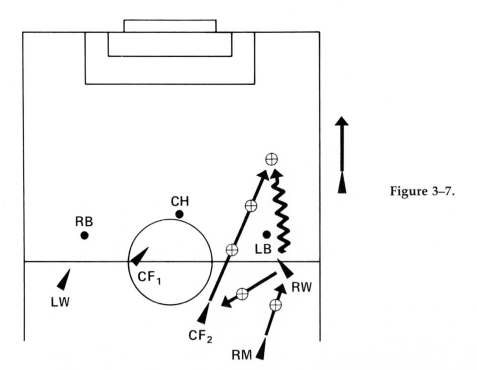

Figure 3–7.

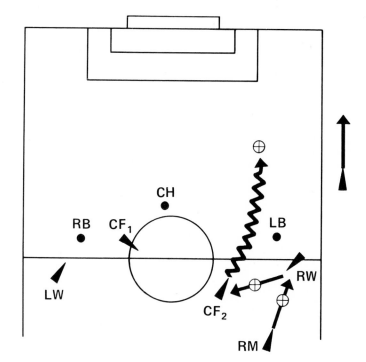

Figure 3–8.

is immediately pressured by defender LB. RW lays off a quick pass to supporting player CF_2. Player CF_2 quickly takes advantage of defenders RB, CH, and LB, by playing a penetrating pass between CH and LB to supporting player RW.

In Figure 3–8, we have the same situation as in Figure 3–7, only this time CF_2 chooses not to pass the ball through the defense. Rather, CF_2 decides to dribble the ball in the direction of defender LB, therefore isolating LB. Then, CF_2 quickly changes direction and penetrates the space between defending players CH and LB.

DELAY IN DEFENSE

The delay in defense tactic allows the team that has lost the ball to set up a deep defensive position. The moment the attacking team loses possession of the ball, they must concern themselves with protecting their own goal. The defending player closest to the ball carrier must delay the carrier's forward progress. This gives the rest of the defending team time to form a deep defensive position. All other defending players will move quickly to the goal side of the ball carrier and other attacking players.

In Figure 3–9, RW moves onto a penetrating pass from CF_1 and puts

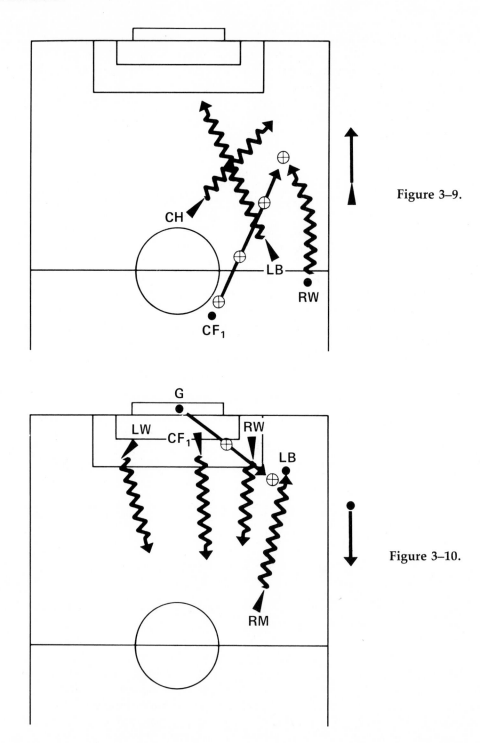

Figure 3–9.

Figure 3–10.

defending players LB and CH momentarily out of the action. Defending player CH moves across to delay attacker RW, allowing LB to cover in depth. It is important that defensive player CH not become committed while LB is trying to recover.

In Figure 3–10, G throws a pass out to attacker LB. The pass catches defending players LW, CF$_1$, and RW in a flat position. Player RM moves immediately to delay LB's forward progress. This frees players LW, CF$_1$, and RW to get goal side of ball carrier LB and give in-depth support to challenger RM.

WIDTH IN ATTACK

For penetrating runs or passes to reach through the opposing team's defense, the principle of width in attack must be applied. Wing play is needed to move defending players into positions without congesting the middle of the field. Players should be encouraged to seek, pass, or dribble the ball into these areas of the field until the defending players commit themselves. Once that happens, penetrating runs and passes must be quick and decisive.

In Figure 3–11, RM has possession of the ball, with players RW and

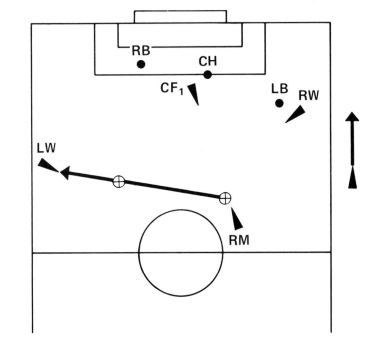

Figure 3–11.

CF in support, but is under pressure from defending players LB and CH. RM decides to pass the ball to supporting player LW, who has maintained width on the far touchline. Defending player RB, who was supporting in depth, now has to decide whether to concede the space out in front to ball carrier LW, or to close down the space to put pressure on LW. In closing down the space, RB runs the risk of getting too far from supporting defenders CH and LB.

CONCENTRATION IN DEFENSE

Concentration in defense is used after other defensive principles have been maintained. When the attacking team occupies a central position in the penalty-area, concentration in defense is most vital. An immediate challenge must be put on the ball carrier. Supporting defenders must close in on attacking players, narrow available space, and restrict possibilities of shots on goal.

In Figure 3–12, RW has possession of the ball in a central position just inside the penalty-area. By applying direct pressure, defender LB forces ball carrier RW to make the next move. Defending players CH and RB, who have applied the principle of concentration, close in on the at-

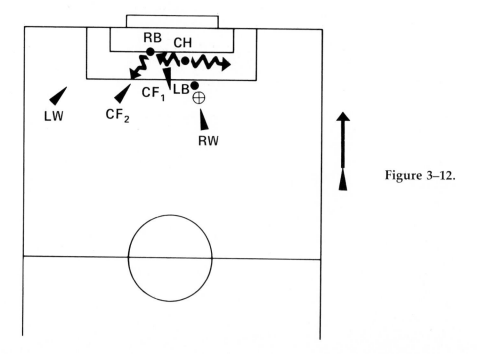

Figure 3–12.

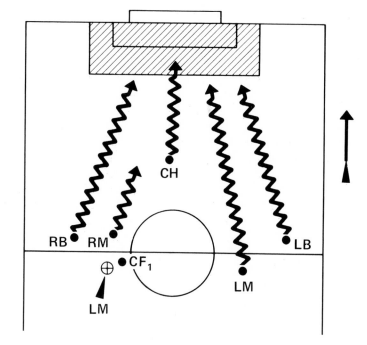

Figure 3–13.

tacking players. Attackers CF, RW, and CF must execute perfectly to score, since defenders LB, CH, and RB have restricted their playing time and available space.

In Figure 3–13, LM possesses the ball and is being delayed by defending player CF_1. Meanwhile, defending players RB, RM, CH, LM, and LB are in full retreat. Yet, they are applying all principles of defense. As they approach their penalty-area they become more concentrated, effectively restricting time and space to prevent shots on goal from central positions. In youth soccer, the greatest percentage of goals and shots on goal come from within the shaded area shown in Figure 3–13.

MOBILITY IN ATTACK

Mobility in attack counteracts the defending team's delay and concentration tactics. Attacking players must interchange positions with and without the ball in an effort to disorganize the defending team. Diagonal runs across and behind defending players are usually the most effective ways of pulling defending players out of position or catching them blindsided. An attacking team with set positions makes the job of defending players easier. The defending player knows immediately which attackers to cover and where to find them during the course of the game. The defending player also quickly becomes acquainted with the strengths and weaknesses of the players covered and compensates accordingly.

In Figure 3–14, RW is in possession of the ball and is supported by attacking players CF_1, CF_2, LM, and LW. Attacking player CF_1 moves into the wing area, drawing along defending player CH. CF_2 holds position and is covered by defending player LM. This leaves space in a central position at the top of the penalty-area. Attacking player LW, seeing this space open up, makes a diagonal run behind defending player RB, and behind defending players RM, LM, and CH. These defensive players are caught watching the ball, concerned only with player movement on the ball side. At the right moment, attacking player LW calls for a through pass from ball carrier RW, for a shot on goal.

In Figure 3–15, attacking player RW has received a pass from RM. RW runs diagonally with the ball, across defending player LB and into a central position at the top of the penalty-area. Here supporting attacking players CF_1 and CF_2 move away. They also try to draw defending players CH and RB toward them. This will free space for RW to shoot, or for a give and go, or for a shot by CF_1 or CF_2, if RW is forced into a passing situation.

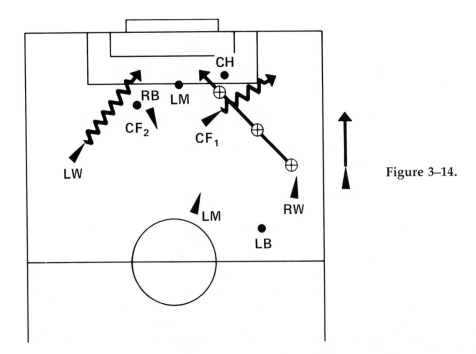

Figure 3–14.

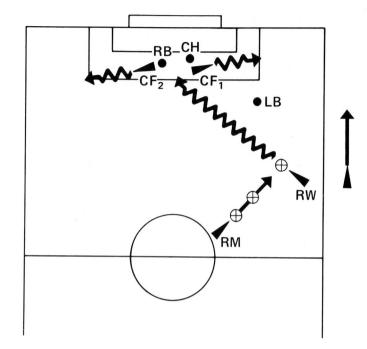

Figure 3–15.

BALANCE IN DEFENSE

Balance in defense must counterbalance mobility in attack. If the interchanging of attacking players is designed to draw defending players out of position, then the defense must be balanced against such moves. Of course this is easier said than done, as young players are easily drawn out of position because they want to be where the ball is, and to kick it. This is fine, as long as training sessions emphasize the importance of balance in defense. It may make the difference between winning and losing a match.

In Figure 3–16, RW has the ball and is supported in depth by attacking players CF_1, CF_2, RM, LM, and LW. However, the defending players have allowed themselves to be drawn out of position and are balanced toward the ball carrier. This has created enough space behind the defense for a pass that gives attacking players LW and LM the opportunity to make a shot or goal.

In Figure 3–17, RW has possession of the ball and is challenged by defending player LB. LB is supported by CH. Defending player RB has moved into a central covering position. RB must direct retreating defensive players RM and LM into areas where concentration and balance can be

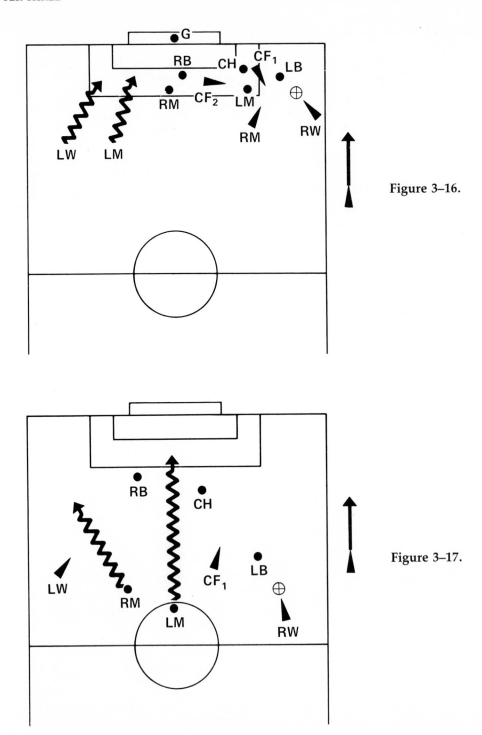

Figure 3–16.

Figure 3–17.

maintained in order to prevent attacking players LW and LM from receiving a cross field pass.

As mentioned in the beginning of this chapter, it is extremely important that the coach and players work hard to apply principles of play in all practice sessions. The first priority should be defense. Cover one principle at a time, and move on to the next one only when players fully understand and can utilize previously taught principles with a certain amount of confidence. (See chapters six through eleven and chapter thirteen for games and drills that reinforce the principles of play in attack.) With young inexperienced players, be very patient. Remember, they want to play soccer because it is a fun game, full of running and kicking. If you reinforce the principles of play before and after each practice, success will be within your grasp.

CHAPTER FOUR

Modern Methods of Coaching

SKILL DEVELOPMENT

Modern methods of coaching concentrate on the soccer player's total skill development. In the past, skill has been defined as high-level individual performance in kicking, heading, passing, and dribbling. Young players growing up in other countries spent many laborious hours teaching themselves techniques associated with their local professional idol. This unsupervised self-teaching resulted in many young players becoming specialists in one aspect of the game. They became known and were recruited for their expertise in one basic skill. Professionally, the player could expect some individual coaching to refine this skill. However, coaching was usually restricted to the functioning of these specialists within the team's style of play. Some coaches argue that there is a need for specialists in today's game, and they are coaching to produce such players. This is fine, as long as the player realizes that this poses limitations on a college or professional soccer career. College and professional soccer teams are looking for soccer players who are highly skilled in the total game. They are looking for versatile players.

TECHNIQUE DEVELOPMENT

Matches or small-sided games must precede the teaching of playing technique. Player and team deficiencies cannot be detected any other way. The English Football Association National Coaching Staff, directed by Alan Wade, and the United States National Coaching Staff, directed by Walter

Chyzowych, stress this point to all their aspiring student coaches. Yet many young players are still submitted to overdoses of technique development sessions. The inexperienced coach either assumes or has been told that perfect technique produces the perfect soccer player. Unfortunately, this is not so. The match or game determines everything. The coach must plan accordingly.

1. *Observation:* During the course of the practice game, if the coach observes players making mistakes, he or she must stop the game and recreate the situation in which the deficiency has occurred.

2. *Organization:* The coach must be prepared and in control at all times. All practice sessions must be realistic, purposeful, and enjoyable. Achievable targets must be set for all players.

3. *Instruction:* When solving a problem, the coach must demonstrate it and either offer or have the players offer alternatives. The demonstration may be a simple walk-through. At this stage there must be a clear, concise, and meaningful understanding of ideas.

4. *Demonstration:* A group of players demonstrates the actual situation, while the coach and other players suggest alternatives. The players must be encouraged to express their own ideas at all times. The coach must be positive and praise the players' efforts to overcome their faults. Constructive criticism is important, but praise and encouragement bring out the best in a player.

GRID SYSTEM OF COACHING

Use of the grid system simplifies organization and control of a large group of players. A grid is simply an area of the playing field or pitch marked out in ten yards square. Most of the sample practices and times given in chapters five through twelve can be adapted to a grid system, with a minimum of two players per grid. The number of players may be increased, if this will aid the development of a specific technique.

The theory behind the grid system of coaching is that all practice situations should prepare players for the game. Therefore, practice sessions should incorporate the essential ingredients of the game. (See the sample layout of a grid system in Figure 4–1.)

A sample coaching session using the grid system follows. In this case, the coach has observed that players are unable to control ground balls.

1. A five-minute small-sided game (six versus six), using forwards against backs, is played.

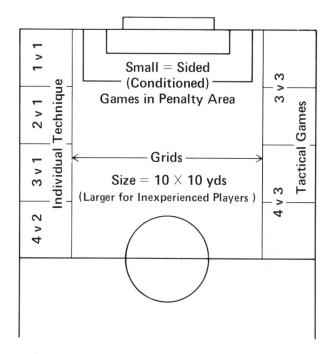

Figure 4–1. Utilizing the grid system for technique and tactical development.

    a. The coach emphasizes the need to control the ball with the sole, inside, and outside of the foot.

    b. The coach stops the game to demonstrate situations in which controlling the ball with the foot can be most effective.

2. The coach demonstrates the technique of controlling the ball with the foot, emphasizing the mechanics of the technique. About three minutes are spent in demonstration.

3. The players pair off, two per grid, and practice passing the ball and controlling it with the sole, inside, or outside of the foot (time: five minutes).

4. The coach divides the players into four per grid (Figure 4–2). Players A, B, C, and D stand in the four corners of the grid. Player A has the ball. A can safely pass the ball to B or C. B and C are standing perpendicular to A. Should A choose to pass the ball to B, diagonally opposite, player C will pressure player B. Player B must control the ball with the foot and then proceed to play three against one until there is a breakdown in play, or until five successful passes have been completed. The players then return to their original corners, and the practice is restarted by another player. Meanwhile, the coach will observe the quality of work in

Figure 4–2. Using the grid practicing for technique with an inside-of-the-foot pass (3 vs. 1).

all the grids and correct any technical errors. This game drill takes ten minutes to complete. If the coach feels further practice is necessary, the drill may be further developed.

5. After a rest or fun game, the players return to the original game of six against six. The coach will continue to screen the play for ball controlling technique with the foot (time: twenty minutes).

CHAPTER FIVE

Ball Juggling

DEVELOPING A FEEL FOR THE BALL

Ball juggling (or ball lifting) is the key to beautiful soccer. It makes players aware of the parts of the body used to control or pass the ball. Gaining a feel for the ball helps players become more confident and imaginative in game play. Of course, the ability to ball juggle indefinitely does not guarantee that players will become the soccer stars of tomorrow. There is no substitute for match play. Ball juggling should precede match practice and take up only a small fraction of the total training session. The coach should encourage players to develop variations in ball juggling technique. The goal is to produce first-class soccer players, not first-class circus performers. When teaching ball juggling techniques, the coach should stress the following points.

1. Before any ball juggling is attempted, players must check the ball for correct air pressure, and make sure that soccer shoelaces are tied neatly at the heel or on the outside of the foot. Failure to check air pressure will lead the player to develop a false sense of feel for the ball. Incorrectly tied laces become a safety hazard.

2. Good players must be "free" of the ball. As long as they have problems controlling the ball, they cannot realize their tactical ideas.

3. Players who want to improve juggling technique in their spare time should practice while stationary, while moving slowly, and while pressured by time or an opponent. Using maximum speed

and power too early in a training program destroys the necessary feel for the ball.

4. To be able to control the ball in different situations, a player must maintain correct body position in relation to the ball.

5. The ball and the human body have different rhythms. The aim of all ball training is to achieve perfect harmony between the player and the ball. The player must try to develop proper technique, and practice outside of regular training sessions whenever possible. Only practice makes perfect, and repetition is the backbone of practice.

BALL JUGGLING WITH THE INSTEP, INSIDE, AND OUTSIDE OF FOOT

Ball juggling with the feet is the most important of all ball juggling techniques. It develops control of ground and air balls, passing, and kicking. Once the technique has been demonstrated, all players should be encouraged to warm up before practice so they can develop the ball juggling sequence.

Instep

The player holds the ball in his or her hands, arms semi-extended in front of the lower chest. The player then drops the ball and, on the bounce, lifts it with the instep back into his or her hands. To lift the ball, the instep and thigh are kept parallel to the ground, with the ankle slightly locked in a downward position. The leg action in this technique is similar to that of a pump or a drum major's step.

Figure 5–1. Instep ball lifting (stationary). *Note:* Position of lifting surface held slightly higher than parallel so as to cradle and lift the ball into the air.

Practice Exercises

a. The players practice in pairs. They face one another, about two yards apart. One player holds a ball at lower chest height and then releases it. When it bounces, this player lifts the ball with the instep back into the air, about chest high. The ball is allowed to bounce once. Then the partner lifts the ball with the instep back into the air. This is repeated. (See Figure 5–1.)

b. Each player holds a ball about waist high and stands on the goal line, facing the penalty-area. On a given signal, the players walk a few paces and then release the ball. When it bounces, the ball is lifted up and slightly forward into the air so that the player can continue walking and playing. When the players reach the front of the penalty-area, they repeat the technique with the opposite foot, continuing back to the goal line. Time used: five minutes. Should players lose control of the ball, they must begin again at the point where control was lost.

c. The players are divided into groups for relays. They line up one behind the other on the goal line. One player stands facing the team, ten yards away, with a ball held between the ankles. On a given signal, the player grips the ball tightly between the ankles and then jumps high and forward like a kangaroo (Figure 5–2). At the highest point, the player

Figure 5–2. Team relay to improve individual player technique ball lifting with the instep.

releases the grip on the ball, allowing it to drop and bounce high enough to lift with the instep. The player must now try to keep the ball in the air with continuous instep lifting until reaching the team. The ball is then lifted to the next person on the team, who controls it with any part of the lower body, grips it between the ankles, and lifts the ball into the air. This player, with continuous instep juggling, returns the ball to the original mark. The player races back to tag the next member of the team, who in turn runs to the ball and repeats the technique. This continues until all members of the team have raced. Any player losing control of the ball must restart from the spot where control was lost. Time used: ten minutes.

Inside of the Foot

The player holds the ball about waist high. The ball is then released. At this moment the player brings the inside of the foot up quickly, lifts the ball back into the air about chest high, and catches it.

Figure 5–3. Inside of the foot ball lifting (stationary). *Note:* Position of the lifting surface is parallel to the ground.

Practice Exercises

a. A player practices the above-described technique, alternating between the left and right foot. Time used: five minutes.

b. Two players face each other, about two yards apart. One player holds a ball chest high. As the pair jogs in the same direction, the player with the ball tosses it about head high. It should bounce high enough for the partner to lift the ball with the inside of the foot back up to the hands. Both players continue to jog, and the technique is repeated. Time used: five minutes.

c. The players practice in groups of three. One player places the ball between the feet. The front of the feet are slightly forward of the midpoint of the ball. With a quick scissor movement of the feet, the ball is popped into the air. The same player now either allows the ball to bounce once first or lifts it immediately with the instep, about upper chest high. The ball is allowed to bounce again, and then one of the other players must lift it with the inside of the foot back into the air. Play continues, with all players lifting the ball with the instep and the inside of the foot. Should the players lose control of the ball, the practice is restarted using the same scissor technique. Time used: ten minutes.

Outside of the Foot

The player holds a ball in one hand. The hand is fully extended out to the side. The ball is then released. At this moment the player directs body weight over the slightly bent supporting leg opposite the extended hand. The player brings up the outside of the playing foot to lift the ball

Figure 5–4. Popping the ball into the air. *Note:* The front inside of both feet are placed either side of the ball. Then with a quick scissor movement of the feet ball pops into the air.

Figure 5–5. Outside of the foot ball lifting (stationary).
Note: Position of the lifting surface is parallel to the ground.

back into the air, about shoulder high, and catches it. The outside of the foot must be parallel to the ground, with the ankle locked in position. (See Figure 5–5.)

Practice Exercises

   a. A player practices the above-described technique, using the outside of both feet. Time used: five minutes.

   b. Players stand on the goal line facing the penalty-area, each holding a ball in one hand. They then walk toward the front of the penalty-area. After a few paces the players release the soccer balls, lift them back into the air with the outside of the foot, and catch them. The players continue to walk and lift the soccer balls until they reach the front of the penalty-area line. Using the other foot, they then go back to the goal line. Time used: five minutes.

   c. The players practice in groups of three. One player stands to the side of a ball, with the outside of the nearest foot approximately two to four inches from it. The player places the opposite foot on top of the ball

Figure 5–6. Popping the ball into the air. *Note:* The front outside of the supporting foot is placed just back from the ball. The ball is then pulled sharply back across the foot causing it to pop into the air.

and pulls it sharply against the outside of the supporting foot, causing the ball to pop into the air. (Figure 5–6.) At this moment the player lifts the ball with the instep into the air, about upper chest high. One of the other players must now attempt to play the ball before it bounces, lifting it with the outside of the foot back into the air about shoulder high. Play continues, with all players using the instep and outside of the foot techniques. If players lose control of the ball, the game is restarted. (See Figure 5–6.) Time used: ten minutes.

BALL JUGGLING WITH THE CHEST AND HEAD

Sometimes it is necessary to use the lofted pass, which requires the ability to control the ball with the thigh, chest, and head. Young and novice players frequently use the lofted pass, although not necessarily by design. Player's lack of experience leads them to rely on this technique. The coach should emphasize controlling the ball with the thigh, chest, and head in his or her training program.

Thigh Juggling

The player holds the ball, arms semi-extended in front of the body. The ball is then released. At this moment the player brings up the thigh to lift the ball back into the air, and then catches it. The thigh must be held

Figure 5–7. Thigh lifting (stationary). *Note:* Position of lifting surface is parallel to the ground.

parallel to the ground directly under the flight of the ball. The ball must play the widest part of the thigh, near the hem of the player's soccer shorts. (See Figure 5–7.)

Practice Exercises

   a. The player practices the technique described above with both the left and the right thigh. Time used: five minutes.

   b. Each player has a ball. They stand on the goal line facing the top of the penalty-area. The players walk a few paces and then toss the balls gently into the air, about head high. At the right moment the players bring up the thighs to lift the balls gently back into the air, and then catch them. The players continue to walk, repeating the technique, until they reach the top of the penalty-area. They then walk back to the goalline repeating this technique, but using the opposite thigh. (See Figure 5–8.) Time used: five minutes.

   c. The players line up for a team relay competition. One player stands facing the team ten yards away with a ball at his or her feet. The player with the ball steps back from it and places the sole of strongest foot on top of the ball. On a given signal, the player pulls the ball sharply back, allowing the foot to follow the contour of the ball so that the backward

Figure 5–8. Practicing for technique thigh lifting (slow moving).

momentum of the ball carries it onto the instep. At this moment the player lifts the ball into the air. He or she allows it to bounce once, and then with an instep volley lifts the ball again, this time in the direction of the team player at the head of the line. According to the service of the ball, this player will now choose either to let the ball bounce once before attempting to thigh juggle, or to thigh juggle the ball before it bounces. This player thigh juggles the ball toward the original ball lifter and tags that player. The first player then sprints to the back of the line. The technique of lifting and juggling the ball is repeated until all team members have participated. (See Figure 5–9.) Time used: ten minutes.

Chest Juggling

The player holds a ball, arms semi-extended and feet astride for balance. The ball is then tossed gently into the air, just above head height. At the right moment the player bends back at the waist and bends the knees to move directly under the ball. With a rocking motion, the player then thrusts the chest up to lift the ball back into the air. The chest must form a platform. The ball is lifted with the breastbone. (See Figure 5–10.)

Figure 5–9a. Basic method preferred for lifting the ball from the ground into the air. *Note:* The leg is semi-extended, with the sole of the foot resting on top of the ball.

Figure 5–9b. The ball is then pulled back sharply and lifted into the air.

Figure 5–10. Ball lifting with the chest (stationary). *Note:* Position of lifting surface is parallel to the ground.

Practice Exercises

a. The player tosses a ball gently into the air, just above head height. The player moves directly under the ball to lift it with the upper chest into the air, then catches it. The player repeats this. Time used: five minutes.

b. The players practice in pairs, facing one another, approximately two yards apart. One player holds the ball. The players then jog in the same direction. The player holding the ball tosses it high enough so that the partner can lift the ball with the chest back into air and then catch it. The players continue to jog and repeat the technique, taking turns tossing and chest lifting the ball. Time used: five minutes.

c. The players practice in groups of three. One player has a ball at the feet. Numbers are assigned to different ball juggling techniques: 1 is lifting with the instep; 2 is lifting with the inside of the foot; 3 is lifting with outside of the foot; 4 is lifting with the thigh; and 5 is lifting with the chest. The player with the ball starts the play by lifting the ball once, letting it bounce, and then lifting it again. At the same time, he or she calls out the next player's name and the number of the next ball juggling technique. The player whose name has been called must attempt to execute the technique. This player will let the ball bounce once and then lift the ball once again with the instep, calling out another name and number. The players must lift the ball high enough so that the next technique can be smoothly executed. Time used: ten minutes.

Figure 5–11. Ball lifting with the forehead (stationary). *Note:* Position of lifting surface is parallel to the ground.

Head Juggling

The player holds the ball in the hands, arms semi-extended, feet astride for balance. The ball is then tossed gently into the air just above head height. The player now throws the head back so that the forehead is parallel to the ground. Bending back at the waist, knees bent, the player moves directly under the flight of the ball and pushes up to meet it and lift it gently back into the air, where it is caught. (See Figure 5–11.)

Practice Exercises

a. The player holds a ball directly out in front of the face, with the arms semi-extended. The player now brings the ball forward and at the same time "throws" the eyes toward the ball, allowing the ball to gently play the forehead. This action is repeated until the player has developed a feeling of confidence and eye-to-ball contact. (See Figure 5–12.) Time used: five minutes.

b. The player holds a ball, arms semi-extended, feet astride for balance. The ball is then tossed gently into the air above head height. The player now moves directly under the ball and with a rocking motion pushes up to meet the ball and lift it back into the air, where it is caught. The player repeats this technique. Time used: five minutes.

Figure 5–12. Practicing for technique, making friends with the soccer ball.

c. The players practice in pairs, facing one another approximately two yards apart. One player holds a ball in the hands, and both players jog in the same direction, with one player jogging backward. The player holding the ball tosses it just above head height. The partner then gently lifts the ball with the forehead and then catches it. The players repeat the technique, taking turns tossing and heading the ball. Time used: five minutes.

d. The players practice in groups of three. One player has a ball at the feet. One foot is placed in front of the ball, with the heel touching it. The other foot is placed behind the ball, with the inside of the foot holding the ball firmly in place. The player pulls the ball with the inside of the foot onto the heel of the supporting foot (Figure 5–13). At this moment, the player snaps the heel up sharply, lifting the ball high in the air and (if possible) over the head (the rainbow, Figure 5–13). Depending on the service, one of the other players will choose either to head the ball immediately or to let it bounce once and then instep lift the ball. The lift must be high enough so that the ball can be headed in turn by each player, until ten consecutive touches have been completed. Should the players lose control of the ball, or should they successfully complete the required number of head juggles, another player will start the game with a rainbow lift.

To conclude the practice session, the coach should encourage the

Figure 5–13a. The rainbow lift. *Note:* The ball rests at the heel of the supporting foot. The ball is then pulled up the back of the supporting leg with the instep of the opposite foot.

Figure 5–13b. The ball is then released and back kicked up and over the player with the original supporting foot.

players to try ball juggling in a sequence such as instep, inside and outside of foot, thigh, head, and chest. As players progress, the coach must set new challenges. Players might practice in small groups and play one touch, using a different technique each time. Players who develop at a slower rate should be encouraged to practice in their spare time.

HOT DOGGING

Every player likes to advertise a touch or feel for the ball. Since it takes time and patience to perfect ball juggling, the player naturally feels

Figure 5–14a. Hot dogging, ball lifting in a sitting position. *Note:* Position of lifting surface is parallel to the ground.

Figure 5–14b. The ball is then lifted gently into the air for practice to dip under to catch and cradle on the neck. *Note:* Position of the head, eyes held up, and neck parallel to the ground.

a great sense of satisfaction and pride in controlling the ball. Ball control was once only expected of foreign players. The following two techniques will give the player a sense of accomplishment.

Instep Ball Juggling in a Sitting Position

The player sits with the knees slightly bent. A ball is held between the ankles, and the player's hands are placed on the ground for support. The player gently tosses the ball into the air with the feet and immediately locks the ankle of the playing foot in a down position. The foot moves directly under the flight of the ball and with the instep lifts the ball back into the air with a pumping action. (See Figure 5–14A).

Catching the Ball on the Neck

The player juggles the ball using different parts of the body. When the ball is completely under control and the player is relaxed, the player gently lifts the ball with the thigh about head high. The player ducks under the ball, bending forward at the waist and bending the knees slightly. At the same time, the player throws the eyes up, forcing the head back and forming a nest at the base of the neck. As soon as the player feels the ball on the neck, the legs give to cushion the impact. Once the ball is dead, the player dips the head, allowing the ball to roll up the back of it. At the right moment, the player snaps the head back sharply to lift the ball into the air. The player continues ball juggling. (See Figure 5–14B.)

CHAPTER SIX

Ball Control

Ball control determines which team will maintain possession of the ball. As soccer becomes more sophisticated, it demands quicker thinking and more precise execution of ball control techniques.

Points to be stressed by the coach include:

1. Whenever possible, the player should move directly into the ball's path.
2. While running the player must decide how to stop the ball. The more skillful the player is, the easier it is for the player to adapt to a situation.
3. The largest possible surface should be used to stop the ball. The controlling surface must be totally relaxed.
4. The moment before impact, the controlling surface should be withdrawn. This will cushion the ball, causing it to stop or drop to the feet.

Common technical mistakes made by players trying to control the ball follow.

1. Players fail to move directly in front of the line of the ball's flight.
2. An opponent's pressure causes the player controlling the ball to lose concentration.
3. The player controlling the ball offers too much resistance, and the ball bounces away.

TRAPPING GROUND BALLS

Young players find it very difficult to stop a rolling ball, especially if they must chase it. Sometimes they run beside the ball, as if they are waiting for it to stop or slow down. Of course, this gives an opponent the chance to steal the ball and pressure the defending players. A player who is trying to stop the ball must be discouraged from using the sole of the foot or back heel stop, unless there are no opponents applying pressure. Many an errant back heel stop has led to a perfect pass to an opposing forward and a shot on goal. There are three basic techniques for stopping ground passes: sole of the foot; inside of the foot; and outside of the foot.

Sole of the Foot

The player moves in front of the ball's path directly facing the passer. The pass should not create lateral movement. Just before contact, the player lifts one leg, balances on the other foot, and locks the ankle in an upward position. The foot must be raised high enough so that the ball wedges between the foot and the ground (cleats toward the ball). The knee is slightly bent, leg relaxed. As the ball strikes the sole of the foot, the player withdraws the foot to cushion impact. (See Figure 6–1.)

Figure 6–1. Controlling a ground ball with the sole of the foot. *Note:* Position of playing foot, heel is close to the ground and cleats are shown to the ball.

Practice Exercises

a. The player stands ten yards from a kickboard. The player underhand rolls a ball against the board. When it rebounds, the player moves forward to meet the ball and controls it with the sole of the foot. Time used: five minutes.

b. Players A and B stand ten yards apart, facing each other. Player A has a ball at the feet. Player A passes the ball to player B and then pressures player B for the ball. Player B moves to meet the ball and control it with the sole of the foot. Then, player B quickly moves laterally with the ball to avoid player A's challenge. Player B dribbles the ball for over ten yards. Time used: ten minutes.

c. Players A, B, and C stand about ten yards apart, forming a triangle. Player A has the ball, and can pass it to player B or player C. If player A passes the ball to player C, player B moves to challenge player C for the ball. Player C must move quickly to meet and control the ball with the sole of the foot. Then, player C passes the ball back to player A, who has moved into a supporting position. Players then alternate positions. Time used: fifteen minutes.

Inside of the Foot

The inside of the foot ball trapping technique is preferred because potential ball receivers are usually sideways on to the ball carrier. It is also

Figure 6–2. Controlling and cushioning a ground ball with the inside of the foot. *Note:* Player receiving the ball is directly behind path of the ball.

Figure 6–3. Controlling a ground ball with the outside of the foot. *Note:* This method is preferred when the player receiving the ball is under extreme pressure of an opponent at the top of an opponent's penalty area.

a fairly easy technique to execute. The player moves in front of the ball's path and directly faces the passer. The player partially locks the ankle in an upward position, with the inside of the foot toward the ball. The knee is slightly bent, leg released. Just before the ball strikes the inside of the foot, the player slides the foot across the body. This cushions and slows the ball's pace. At the same time, the player turns away from the passer. The ball is cradled to a stop and held between the inside of the foot and the ground.

Practice Exercises

a. With a ball at the feet, player A faces player B, who is ten yards away. Player A passes the ball to player B, who stops the ball with the inside of the foot (Figure 6–2). Players A and B alternate controlling and passing the ball. Time used: five minutes.

b. Five players position themselves around the center circle, an equal distance apart from one another. One player has the ball and can pass it to any one of the four supporting players. Once the pass has been made, the passer follows the ball. The receiver controls the ball with the inside of the foot, passes the ball to another player, and then follows the ball. Time used: six minutes.

c. Player A, with a ball at the feet, stands at the top corner of the penalty-area, facing the center line. Player B stands twenty yards away, facing player A. Player C stands behind player B, arms fully extended, hands on player B's shoulders. Player B moves quickly toward player A, hoping to catch player C off guard and receive a pass from player A. Player B must control the ball with the inside of the foot and pass the ball back to player A while under heavy pressure from player C. Players A and B play "keep away control and pass soccer" until player C intercepts the ball or five passes are completed. The players then rotate. Time used: twelve minutes.

Outside of the Foot

Modern-day soccer demands that the soccer player move unpredictably to keep an opponent off balance. Stopping a ball with the outside of the foot is one technique that is used to surprise an opponent. The player who continually controls ground passes with the same technique and then always moves in the same direction becomes easy prey for an opponent. On the other hand, the striker who stops the ball with the outside of the foot, "spins off" an opponent, and cuts back in toward the goal will bewilder and outwit an opponent.

When executing this technique, the player moves directly in front of the ball's path. At the right moment, the player partially locks the ankle down, toes forced in, showing the outside of the foot to the ball. The knee is slightly bent, leg relaxed. Just before the ball strikes the outside of the foot, the player withdraws the foot to cushion and slow the pace of the ball. (See Figure 6–3.)

Practice Exercises

a. Player A, with a ball at the feet, stands ten yards away from player B. Player A passes the ball to player B, who controls the ball with the outside of the foot. Players A and B alternate passing and controlling the ball. Time used: five minutes.

b. The players are divided into two teams. One team stands on the touchline between the goal line and the center line, with players five yards apart. Each player has a ball at the feet. The other team lines up ten yards away. On a given signal, players move slowly along the touchline toward the goal line or the center line, passing the ball with their partner, using the outside of the foot. Players change direction when they reach either the goal line or the center line. As players pass other players moving in the opposite direction, they must concentrate on their ball and on supporting player (teammate) moving off the ball. Time used: six minutes.

c. Player A with a ball at the feet, stands on one side of the center circle. Supporting player B stands on the opposite side of the circle, facing player A. Player B is closely marked by defending player C. Player A passes the ball on either side of supporting player B, causing lateral or diagonal movement. Player B, closely marked by defending player C, moves quickly toward the ball as if to carry it in the same direction. At the right moment, player B controls the ball with the outside of the foot, "spins off" player C, and moves toward the center of the field. Time used: twelve minutes.

CONTROL OF AIR BALLS

Long clearances and chipped passes over opponents are sometimes needed to relieve or apply pressure. The receiving or challenging player must be able to control the air ball to maintain or regain ball possession. A lack of playing experience is the major reason why novice players have difficulty controlling the ball. They usually wait for the ball to bounce two or three times—and the ball is stolen by an opponent. Or sometimes they treat the ball like a "hot potato" and kick it with might and fury.

There are many techniques used to control an air ball, both conventional and unconventional. In any case, the principles of ball control are the same. The player must move into the ball's path, decide how to control the ball, and make sure that the controlling surface is relaxed and slightly withdrawn upon contact.

In this section, eight techniques for controlling air balls are discussed. They range from the basic sole foot trap to the more advanced progressive toe trap.

Sole of the Foot Trap

Controlling an air ball with the sole of the foot is one of the first techniques the young player is encouraged to perfect. Proper execution of this technique causes a player to move toward the ball and eliminates the possibility of a ball bouncing out of reach. When executing this technique, the player moves directly into the ball's line of flight. The moment the ball strikes the ground, the player lifts the foot, ankle partially locked in an upward position, with the sole of the foot in front of the ball. The knee is slightly bent and the leg relaxed. Proper execution should cause the ball to have backspin.

Practice Exercises

a. The player holds the ball and stands three yards from a kickboard. The player throws the ball underhand at the kickboard. The ball should

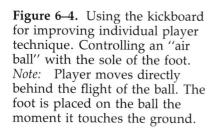

Figure 6–4. Using the kickboard for improving individual player technique. Controlling an "air ball" with the sole of the foot. *Note:* Player moves directly behind the flight of the ball. The foot is placed on the ball the moment it touches the ground.

be thrown at head height and hard enough to strike the ground in front of the player. The player moves directly toward the flight of the ball and sole foot traps the ball. This exercise is repeated over and over. (See Figure 6–4.) Time used: five minutes.

    b. Player A holds the ball. Player B stands about five yards away, facing player A. The players jog in the same direction. Player A throws the ball gently into the air. Player B pauses, then moves forward and sole foot traps the ball. Once the ball has been controlled, player B gathers the ball up, and both players begin jogging again. This time, player B throws the ball for player A to control. Time used: six minutes.

    c. Player A stands outside of the touchline, with the ball held in a throw-in position. Player B stands ten to twelve yards inside the field of play, closely marked by player C. Player A takes the throw-in, aiming the ball at supporting player B's feet. Player B, pressured by player C, moves directly into the line of the ball's flight and controls it with the sole of the foot. Players A and B keep the ball away from player C until it is intercepted or five passes have been completed. Players then alternate. Time used: twelve minutes.

Inside of the Foot Trap

    Most players prefer to use the inside of the foot trap when they receive an air ball from a central position into the wing area. Proper execution of this technique allows a player to control the ball and move fluidly

Figure 6–5. Controlling an air ball with the inside of the foot. *Note:* The moment the ball touches the ground the player controls it with the inside of the foot.

away from defending players. For example, a goalkeeper throws an air ball to a supporting player, just beyond the top of the penalty-area and near the touchline. The receiver moves directly toward the ball. The moment the ball strikes the ground, the player lifts the foot, knee slightly bent, leg relaxed, ankle partially locked upward. The inside of the foot is wedged behind the ball and controls it. The player pivots and sweeps the ball across the body in one motion. (See Figure 6–5.)

Practice Exercises

   a. The player holds the ball extended in the hand that is opposite the intended playing foot. The player releases the ball, pivots, and controls it with the inside of the foot. The player sweeps the ball in the opposite direction. Time used: five minutes.

   b. Player A holds the ball. Player B stands five yards away, facing player A. The players move across the field. Player A gently throws the ball toward player B. The moment the ball strikes the ground, player B pivots, controls the ball, and sweeps it in the opposite direction. Player B speed dribbles with the ball over five yards. The technique is repeated. Time used: eight minutes.

c. Players A, B, and C stand ten yards apart, forming a triangle. Player A can throw the ball to either player B or player C. If player A throws the ball to supporting player C, player B will become a defender and apply immediate pressure. Player C, using the inside of the foot trap, must move the ball away from defending player B. Players A and C will play two-touch soccer until player B intercepts the ball or five passes have been completed. The players then switch. Time used: twelve minutes.

Outside of the Foot Trap

Most players prefer the outside of the foot technique when receiving an air ball from a central position in the wing area. Properly executed, this technique catches a close-marking opponent off balance. It also allows the ball carrier to cut infield to the defender's weak side. A typical situation would evolve from a throw-in. The ball is thrown toward the supporting player's feet. This player moves directly toward the ball. The moment before the ball hits the ground, the player lifts the playing foot and partially locks the ankle upward and away from the supporting foot. As soon as the ball strikes the ground, the outside of the foot traps the ball and simultaneously sweeps it back across the body. The knee is slightly bent and the leg relaxed.

Practice Exercises

a. The player holds the ball in one hand, on the same side of the body as the intended playing foot. The player releases the ball, pivots, controls it with the outside of the foot, and sweeps it in the opposite direction. Time used: five minutes.

b. Players A and B stand on opposite sides of the center circle, facing each other. Player A holds the ball and full instep volley kicks it toward player B. Player B moves directly toward the ball. When the ball strikes the ground, player B executes the outside of the foot trap. Player B dribbles the ball back to the center circle and one-fourth of the distance around it. Player B full instep volley kicks the ball to player A, who has moved around the circle and is standing opposite. Player A repeats the technique. Time used: six minutes.

c. Six players stand equidistant around the center circle. One more player stands in the middle of the circle. Five of the six players around the circle have balls. The coach assigns the numbers to the various techniques: 1 is sole foot trap; 2 is inside of the foot trap; 3 is outside of the foot trap. One player starts the practice either by taking a throw-in or by full instep volley kicking the ball toward the player in the center of the circle. While kicking or throwing the ball, the player will call out a number.

Figure 6–6. Controlling an air ball with the outside of the foot. *Note:* The player moves directly behind the flight of the ball. The moment the ball touches the ground the player pivots and controls the ball with the outside of the foot.

The player in the center of the circle must execute the corresponding technique. Once the ball has been controlled, it is passed to the player who did not have a ball when practice began. The player in the center circle must be kept busy. Players change every forty-five seconds. Total time used: twenty minutes.

Toe Trap

The toe trap is a relatively new technique. This technique is very useful when a ball drops vertically and has only limited forward and backward movement. Any high head ball that finds the player with a limited amount of pressure would call for a toe trap. The player moves directly into the line of the ball's flight. Before the ball strikes the ground, the player slides the front of the foot under the ball. Both the leg and the foot should be totally relaxed. The moment the ball makes contact with the front of the foot, the player gently slides the foot back causing the ball to back spin and stop.

Practice Exercises

a. Players are divided into teams for a relay competition. A team captain stands five yards in front of and facing his or her team, holding a ball. On a given signal, the team captain throws the ball toward the player at the head of the line. This player controls the ball with the toe. The player turns, dribbles the ball down one side of the team and back along the other side, and tags and replaces the team captain. The team

Figure 6–7. Controlling an air ball with the toes (toe trap). *Note:* The players move directly behind the flight of the ball. The controlling foot is held close to the ground and relaxed causing the ball to "die" on contact.

captain races to the back of the line. The relay continues until the team captain is back in front of the team. (See Figure 6–7.) Time used: nine minutes.

b. Players A and B practice with a goalkeeper. Player A stands at the top of the penalty-area with a ball at the feet. Player B stands at the top corner of the penalty-area. Player A dribbles the ball toward the penalty spot and shoots it at the goalkeeper. The goalkeeper makes a save and immediately punts the ball in the direction of player B. The moment the goalkeeper punts the ball, player A pressures player B. Player B executes a toe trap, turns away from the goal, and speed dribbles ten to fifteen yards downfield. Players A and B alternate. Time used: twelve minutes.

Progressive Toe Trap

The progressive toe trap is similar to controlling the ball with the front of the foot. The differences are as follows. First, the trajectory of the ball is less vertical. Second, the approach is better suited to situations in which the ball is traveling from a central into a wing position. Third, on contact with the front of the foot, the ball is "killed" and gently carried through the player's legs in one motion (Figure 6–8). The player "spins off" and dribbles the ball downfield.

A cross field lofted pass to a winger might set up a progressive toe tap. The winger moves directly into the line of the ball's flight, while under pressure from an opponent on the goal side. Right before the ball bounces, the winger slides the contact surface (his or her foot) under the ball. Once

Figure 6–8. Controlling an air ball with the toes (progressive toe trap). *Note:* Same as Figure 6–7 except when ball plays the foot, the foot is drawn back with ball sitting on the front of it. The player now spins in the direction of the supporting foot to collect and move down field.

the ball strikes the front of the foot, the winger carries it through the legs, spins off the challenger, and dribbles the ball downfield.

Practice Exercises

Use the exercises described previously for practicing the regular toe trap.

Instep Trap (Pulling the Ball Down)

The instep trap, like the toe trap, is very useful when the ball is dropping vertically. The player moves directly in line with the ball's flight and raises the controlling foot up to meet it. The ankle is semi-locked in an upward position, the leg is extended, knee bent, and the thigh held a little higher than horizontal. The moment the ball strikes the instep, the foot is lowered. This brings the ball gently to the ground. (See Figure 6–9.)

Practice Exercises

a. The player tosses a ball forward into the air and then moves directly toward it. The player raises the foot to catch the ball on the instep.

Figure 6–9. Controlling an air ball with the instep. *Note:* The player moves directly behind the flight of the ball. The playing foot is then lifted up to meet the ball. The moment the ball plays the foot the ball is lowered to the ground.

When the ball strikes the contact surface, the ankle, foot, and leg relax in order to cushion the ball's impact. Time used: five minutes.

b. The players practice in pairs. The ball carrier stands on the touchline. The partner stands five yards away, facing the ball carrier. The players jog in the direction of the opposite touchline. (One player jogs backward.) The player with the ball tosses it toward the partner, who moves into the line of the ball's flight and pulls it down with the instep.

c. This exercise is similar to exercise b. The player holds the ball in a regular throw-in position, and the partner stands ten yards away. On a given signal, the player with the ball takes a regular throw-in in the direction of the partner and then follows the ball. The partner must control the ball with the instep and dribble past the oncoming player, who will challenge for the ball. The players then change places. Time used: ten minutes.

Thigh Trap

Controlling the ball with the thigh usually suggests that the player has time and space, has moved quickly toward the ball, and has been caught by a surprise pass. For example, a lofted pass might find a player unmarked. The player moves directly toward the ball and raises the thigh under the falling ball. The moment the ball strikes, the thigh gives to

Figure 6–10. Controlling an air ball with the thigh. (See also Figure 5–7.) *Note:* The player moves directly behind the flight of the ball. The thigh is then lifted up to meet the ball. The moment the ball plays the thigh it is lowered causing the ball to drop at the feet.

cushion the impact. The leg is lowered, allowing the ball to fall to the ground. (See Figure 5–7, page 46.)

Practice Exercises

a. The player tosses a ball into the air and quickly moves toward it. At the right moment, the player executes a thigh trap, causing the ball to fall to the ground. (See Figure 6–10.) Time used: five minutes.

b. The players are divided into teams for a relay competition. Team captains stand ten yards in front of and facing their respective teams, holding the ball in a regular throw-in position. All other team members are in a sitting position, with their legs crossed. On a given signal, each team captain throws the ball toward the team player sitting at the head of the line. The moment the ball is thrown, the sitting player stands up, moves toward the ball and executes a thigh trap. Once the ball strikes the ground, the player executes a sole of the foot trap. The player dribbles the ball forward, then tags and replaces the team captain. The captain runs and sits at the back of the team. The relay continues until the team captain is back at the front of the team. Time used: fifteen minutes.

c. Player A holds a ball in a regular throw-in position. Player B stands ten yards in front of player A. Player C stands fifteen yards in front of A. Players B and C both face A. Player A throws the ball toward player B, so that it can be controlled with the thigh. Player B executes a thigh trap. After allowing the ball to drop, player B side foot traps the ball, turns and dribbles toward player C. The moment player B establishes ground control, player A races toward player C. Player A must prevent player B from playing the ball through the legs of player C for a goal. Players then change positions. Time used: twelve minutes.

Chest Trap

The chest trap is very popular because if it is properly executed and time and space allow, the player is free to dribble, pass, or turn in the opposite direction with the ball. The advantage of using the chest trap instead of heading or volley kicking is that the team is more likely to maintain ball possession.

There are two techniques that the player must perfect. One is used for air balls that result from lofted passes dropping vertically, and the other is for balls that are line driven at about chest height. Take, for example, a lofted kick (punt) from the goalkeeper to a supporting forward

Figure 6–11. Controlling an "air ball" (line drive) with the chest. *Note:* Position "V" shape causing the ball to be pushed down to the ground.

player. The player moves directly into the line of the ball's flight and at the right moment places one foot (astride) behind the other, pushes up on the toes, straightens the legs, and thrusts the chest up under the ball. The moment the ball strikes the chest, the player relaxes the body, bending at the knees and rocking softly back on the heels to cushion the ball's impact.

Any misdirected shot on goal or panic clearance that finds a player directly in the ball's path calls for a chest trap. The player acts immediately, withdrawing the hips and placing one foot backward, so that, sideways, the body resembles the letter V. Straight-legged, the player raises the chest above the midpoint of the ball, pushing it down toward the ground. (See Figure 6–11.)

Practice Exercises

a. The player stands three yards from a kickboard or some other flat surface. The player throws the ball high against the kickboard, so that the ball drops vertically. The player moves toward the ball, and executes a chest trap. Time used: five minutes.

b. The player forcefully underhand pitches the ball against the kickboard, moves directly toward it, and then withdraws the hips and one foot until, seen sideways, the body forms a V. The player raises the chest above the ball, pushing the ball toward the ground. Time used: five minutes.

c. The players are divided into teams for a relay competition. They stand in a line behind the touchline. A team captain stands ten yards in front of each team, facing the team, legs apart, holding a ball in a regular throw-in position. On a given signal, each team captain throws the ball to the player at the head of the line. This player controls the ball with the chest and allows it to drop. When the ball lands, the player executes a sole of the foot trap. The player dribbles forward, passes, and then follows the ball through the team captain's legs to replace and repeat. The team captain runs to the back of the line. The relay continues until the team captain once again heads the team. (See Figure 6–12.) Time used: eighteen minutes. Note: To teach control of a low horizontal pass with the chest trap, have the team captain pitch the ball underhand while standing five yards away.

d. Eight field players and a goalkeeper practice together. One player stands at the top of the penalty-area, facing the center line. The other players stand twenty yards away in a semi-circle, equally spaced across the width of the field. These players are numbered one through seven. Odd-numbered players hold balls in their hands; even-numbered players

Figure 6–12. Team relays to improve individual player technique.

have balls at their feet. Starting from the left, the first player full instep volley kicks the ball in a retaining arc toward the player on his or her right. The receiving player controls the ball with the chest, allows it to drop, executes an inside or outside of the foot trap, and then shoots directly at the goalkeeper. The receiving player returns to starting position and receives a hard low pass from the second player. All players take turns controlling the ball. Time used: thirty minutes. Note: The goalkeeper may challenge the ball carrier.

Head Trap

The head trap is the most difficult technique to perform. As with the chest trap, two procedures must be mastered: one for air balls dropping vertically; and one for horizontal line drives that are head high. Very few players use the head trap. If they use another method, players are more confident that they will be able to move the ball after they have trapped it.

The head trap might be used to control an air ball that has dropped sharply from a full instep volley kick. The player moves directly under the ball and then jumps up on one foot to meet it. The ball should strike the forehead at the exact moment when the player has reached maximum height. Both the ball and player descend together. The moment the player's feet strike the ground, knees bend and the body relaxes to cushion impact.

Practice Exercises

a. The player practices with a tether ball. The ball is tied to a cross bar so that it touches the player's forehead when the player stands in front of the ball. The player puts one foot behind the other and pushes the ball gently forward. When it swings back, the player moves sideways underneath the ball. The eyes are thrown up to meet the ball. When it touches the forehead, the player withdraws the head and body in a rocking motion to cushion impact. (See Figure 6–13.) Time used: five minutes.

b. Player A stands on the touchline holding a ball. Player B sits ten yards away facing player A. Player A throws the ball high into the air toward player B. The moment the ball has been thrown, player B stands up and moves toward it. Player B makes a one-footed vertical jump to meet the ball and executes a head trap. Player B then allows the ball to drop and executes one of the three basic foot traps. The practice resumes with player B throwing the ball to player A. (See Figure 6–14.) Time used: six minutes.

c. Player A holds the ball. Player B stands five yards away. Player C stands twelve yards away. They form a straight line facing player A. Player A throws the ball to player B. Player B executes a head trap, fol-

Figure 6–13. Utilizing the tether ball for improving individual player technique. Controlling an "air ball" with the forehead. *Note:* The player moves directly behind the flight of the ball and at the moment of contact draws the head back causing the ball to stop.

Figure 6–14. Controlling an "air ball" with the forehead while under pressure of an opponent.

lowed by a thigh trap and a sole of the foot trap. As soon as player A throws the ball, player C executes a forward roll, stands up, and challenges player B. Players A and B play two-touch soccer until five passes have been completed or until player C wins possession of the ball. Players change positions. (See Figure 6–14.) Time used: twelve minutes. Note: Distance between players A and C may vary according to the players' execution of the head trap.

CHAPTER SEVEN

Passing Is the Name of the Game

As every soccer fan knows, "Passing is the name of the game"; "If you can't pass, you can't play." Every coach tries to develop the players' passing skills. Players who deftly pass the ball back and forth work together as a team. And you can't win a soccer game without teamwork.

When dealing with young novice players, a coach need not be concerned with mechanics and technique. The coach should merely make sure that players can competently pass the ball with any part of the foot in such a way that a teammate can easily receive and control the ball.

Playing experience, continual reinforcement, and developing passing technique in practice sessions will help players accept passing over dribbling as a much safer and faster way of moving the ball downfield. Since the ball travels faster than a person, one timely, accurate through pass may eliminate two to ten defending players.

There are two types of passes that use the feet: ground passes and lofted or chipped passes. Ground passes range in distance from five to forty yards. Lofted or chipped passes range in distance from ten to fifty yards.

GROUND PASSES

The ball can be passed with any part of the foot. But the player must master passing with the inside of the foot, the outside of the foot, and the instep before attempting other passes. The coach must stress the following points about ground passing techniques.

1. To keep the ball on the ground, the contact surface must strike the ball at its midline, or just above.

2. The player's eyes and center of balance must be directly over the ball.

3. The foot's contact surface must push and follow through to achieve accuracy.

4. The pass's timing and power must coincide with the intended receiver's proximity to the passer and with the time and space allowed by the receiver's opponent.

5. The nonkicking foot must be next to the ball, pointing at the target.

One common mistake a player may make is to have his or her center of balance behind the ball. This can cause the following errors.

1. The player strikes the ball below the midline and lifts it into the air.

2. The player's leg swings across the ball, instead of through it.

3. The pass lacks power.

Inside of the Foot

The inside of the foot pass is the most common of all the ground passing techniques. When the contact surface is the largest area on the foot, the technique has greater accuracy and is easier to execute. A prime time to use this procedure would be if a wing fullback wanted the ball to reach a supporting winger twenty yards away. The fullback would directly approach the ball, face the winger, and execute an inside of the foot pass to the winger.

Practice Exercises

a. The player places a target, such as a cone or cardboard box, in front of a kickboard. The player stands approximately ten yards in front of the kickboard, with a ball at his or her feet. The player approaches the ball. On the last step of the approach, the player places the nonpassing foot beside the ball, with the knee slightly bent. The player's center of balance and eyes are directly over the ball. The passing foot is one pace behind the ball, leg straight, with the inside of the foot nearly at a right angle to the nonpassing foot. The player raises the passing foot backwards from the hip, bending the knee slightly at the same time. Arms are extended for balance. With a quick downward swing of the leg, the inside of the foot strikes the ball around the midline and follows up and through

Figure 7–1a. Passing the ball along the ground using the inside of the foot. *Note:* The supporting foot is placed along side of the ball for direction. Player's body weight is directly over the ball. The striking foot is drawn back and balance is maintained.

Figure 7–1b. The striking foot is then brought forward with the side of the foot at right angles to the supporting foot. The foot plays the ball and follows through.

in one fluid motion. This causes top spin and ensures that the ball stays low. (See Figures 7–1 a and b.) Time used: five minutes.

   b. Players pair off and stand along the touchline, ten yards apart and facing each other. One player side foot passes the ball to his or her

Figure 7–2. Practicing for technique 5 v 2 inside of the foot passing.

partner. The partner controls the ball with any part of the foot and then returns the pass. Players compete for the most accurate passing performance. Time used: six minutes.

c. Seven players practice together. Five players stand around the center circle, an equal distance apart. Two defending players stand in the circle. Practice begins when an offensive player inside of the foot passes the ball to a supporting player. The receiver controls the ball and then inside of the foot passes while being pressured by a defender. Defenders change every time there is an interception or an errant pass. (See Figure 7–2.) Time used: twenty minutes.

Outside of the Foot

The outside of the foot pass is frequently displayed by South American and European players. It has added flair to the game of soccer. To some extent, the outside of the foot pass has given the one-footed player the same offensive threat as the two-footed player. Proper execution at the right moment can take one's opponent by surprise and create an off-balance situation in the defense. For example, a winger dribbles the ball and takes on the opposing fullback. Suddenly the winger cuts, turning the fullback inside, to create attacking space in the wing area. The winger then executes an outside of the foot pass into the path of an overlapping supporting player who has enough space to move with a certain amount of composure.

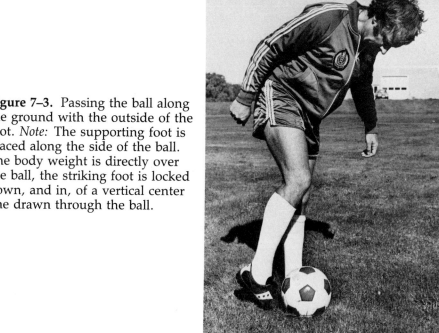

Figure 7–3. Passing the ball along the ground with the outside of the foot. *Note:* The supporting foot is placed along the side of the ball. The body weight is directly over the ball, the striking foot is locked down, and in, of a vertical center line drawn through the ball.

Practice Exercises

a. Player A stands one step away from the ball. Player B stands ten yards away, facing player A. Player A approaches the ball as if to make an inside of the foot pass. However, as the passing foot is raised backwards, the foot is forced in, and the ankle locked down (Figure 7–3). Player A strikes the ball around the midline and follows through. This causes the ball to travel with top spin to player B. The ball is controlled by player B, and the technique is repeated. Time used: five minutes.

b. Players A, B, and C stand ten yards apart on the touchline, facing the opposite touchline. Player A stands in the middle. Player A dribbles the ball in the direction of the opposite touchline, supported by player B on the right and player C on the left. After dribbling for about five yards, player A executes an outside of the foot lead pass to player B (Figure 7–4). This time, however, player A places the nonpassing foot further away from the ball. This allows enough space for the passing foot to strike the inside of the ball and play it laterally and forward with the outside of the foot. Player B controls the ball and then makes a forward diagonal run to

Figure 7–4. Practicing for technique outside of the foot in groups of three "pass-and-follow."

interchange with player A. Player B continues to dribble the ball toward the touchline and executes an outside of the foot pass to player C with the left foot. The ball is controlled by player C, who dribbles the ball diagonally forward to interchange with player B. The technique is continued until the opposite touchline is reached. Time used: ten minutes.

c. Players A and B are attackers, and C and D are defenders. Player A stands at the center spot, facing the goal. The ball lies at his or her feet. Player B stands on the center line approximately thirty yards away from player A. Player C stands on the center circle ten yards away and faces player A. Player D man marks player B. Player A dribbles the ball toward, and then diagonally away from, supporting player, pulling defending player C out of a central covering position. At this moment, supporting attacker B makes a diagonal run into the space vacated by player C. Player B receives an outside of the foot pass from attacking player A and then attempts to score, while being pressured by defending player D. Players then change positions. Time used: twenty minutes. (See Figure 7–5.)

Instep (Through Pass)

The through pass, more commonly referred to as the "killer pass," is probably the most difficult pass to deliver because it demands great timing and accuracy. The through pass is most effective when the defending team has failed to apply the principles of concentration and balance, especially in the preparation area (midfield).

The instep through pass would be "on" in the following situation.

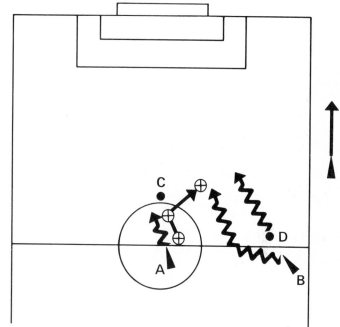

Figure 7–5. Functional training for technique outside of the foot pass.

A striker is standing near the center line facing his or her own goal. The striker receives a pass and lays the ball back to a supporting midfielder. The midfielder fakes a pass to the near supporting winger, spins off, and faces the opposite supporting winger. The opposing fullback, who has been covering in depth, anticipates a cross field pass and races to close in on the winger. At this moment the midfielder executes an instep through pass past the fullback to the supporting winger. The winger runs for the ball and dribbles toward the opponent's goal for a shot.

After the approach stage, this technique differs in only a few ways from the inside of the foot pass. First, when the leg swings downward, the player's foot is slightly open. Second, leg action is faster; knee action is like a whip. Third, the instep (along the inside of the laces) strikes the ball. Fourth, the ankle, knees, and eyes are forced down on the follow-through.

Practice Exercises

a. One player stands at the top corner of the penalty-area, with a ball at the feet. The other player stands at the opposite top corner of the penalty-area, forty-four yards away. The player with the ball takes two or three paces back from the ball, stepping off to the side in an arc. The player approaches the ball from an angle. The player's instep strikes the

Figure 7–6. Instep ground pass over 20–30 yards. *Note:* Supporting foot gives the direction, body weight directly over the ball and striking foot locked down.

ball's midline. After gaining ball control, the second player repeats the technique. (See Figure 7–6.) Time used: five minutes.

    b. Seven players form a circle approximately forty yards in diameter. On a given signal, four of the players instep pass balls to receiving players. The receivers quickly control these balls and instep pass them to other players. Players must observe other team players and their intended passes at all times. If balls collide on the way to a receiver or if a receiver has more than one soccer ball to control, the guilty parties must run one full lap of the circle. (See Figure 7–7.) Time used: twelve minutes.

    c. Attackers A and B, defenders C and D, and a goalkeeper practice together. Attacker A stands at the bottom of the center circle, closest to the goalkeeper. Attacker B stands on the center line, near a touchline. Defensive player C stands at the top of the center circle in the other half of the field. Defensive player D man marks attacker B. The goalkeeper starts the practice by volley kicking the ball to attacker A. As soon as attacker A controls the ball, defensive player C applies strong pressure. As soon as attacker A turns with the ball, supporting attacker B calls for a through pass to the inside of defensive player D. Attacker A responds by driving an instep pass through the space for attacker B. Attacker B collects the ball and dribbles into the opposite penalty-area while being pressured by defensive player D. All field players then change positions. Time used: twenty minutes. (See Figure 7–8.)

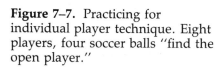

Figure 7–7. Practicing for individual player technique. Eight players, four soccer balls "find the open player."

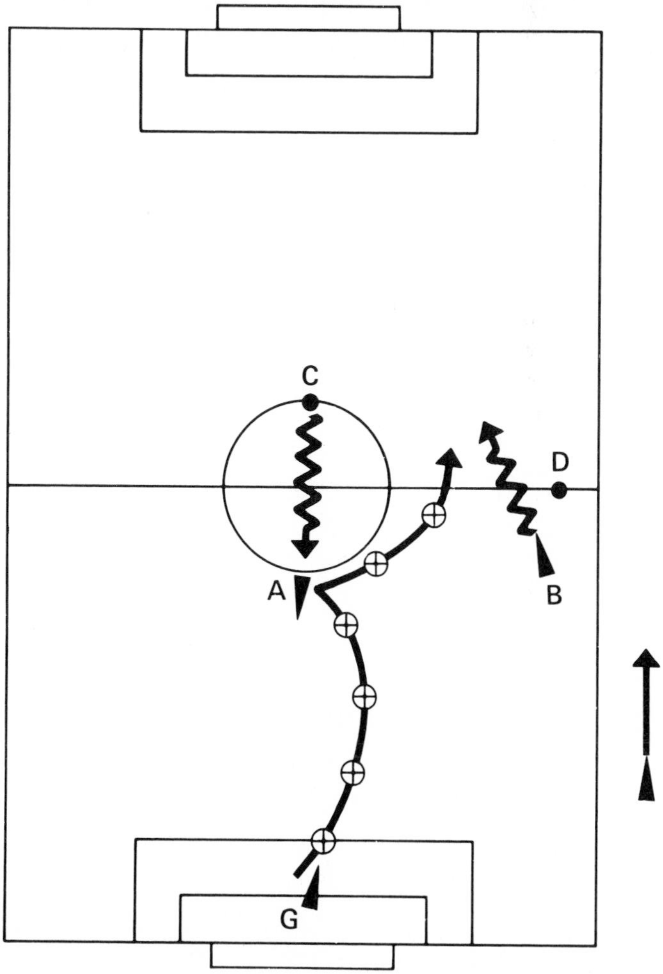

Figure 7–8. Functional training for technique instep through pass.

LOFTED AND CHIPPED PASSES

Lofted Pass

The lofted pass is usually used to surprise an opponent. It requires accuracy, good timing, and control. Unfortunately, some young players and coaches confuse the lofted pass with the lofted kick. The lofted pass has direction and an intended receiver. The lofted kick, on the other hand, has no direction and is up for grabs, so to speak. The sad thing is that many of these aimless kicks bounce in favor of the attacking team. After all, young novice players often cannot control air balls or head the ball. Goals are scored, games are won, and everybody loses for nobody experiences the true nature of the game.

When teaching the lofted pass, the coach should stress the following points. You will notice that these rules differ from those given for the ground pass.

1. To lift the ball, the contact surface must strike the ball below the ball's midline.
2. The nonkicking foot is placed to the side of and behind the ball.
3. Body weight, center of balance, and eyes are behind the ball.
4. The instep is used; the ankle is locked down.
5. The player approaches the ball on an angle.
6. The last step of the player's approach should be a long one.
7. The swing of the player's leg should be as long as possible.
8. The player's knee straightens before contact.

Problems commonly encountered when executing the lofted pass are as follows.

1. The player pulls the ball and loses accuracy. What causes this? The player's approach to the ball is too straight, the ball is hit off-center, or the player allows the kicking foot to follow around, rather than through, the ball.
2. The player's pass has height and accuracy but no power. This could be because the player's nonkicking foot is positioned too far behind the ball. As a result the body weight does not follow through the kicking movement. The player must stretch and kick *at* the ball, rather than *through* it.
3. The player's pass loses height. Lack of concentration can cause this problem: a head is lifted, eyes are taken off the ball. Or a

player may allow body weight and balance to be directed in too vertical a plane. This restricts the leg's high follow-through.

4. The player who lifts the ball too steeply, too soon, is sweeping *under* the ball and lifting in too vertical a plane. The ball should be driven *through* a horizontal plane.

The lofted pass is an ideal counterattacking weapon. Your half of the field is congested. You can't use the short pass. It's time to loft the ball over defending players and reach your strikers.

For example, the lofted pass might be ''on'' in the following situation. After making a save from a corner kick, the goalkeeper quickly propels the ball to the supporting winger on the lean side of the field, just outside the penalty-area. The winger controls the ball, turns, and executes a lofted pass over the challenging fullback into the wing area toward a striker.

Practice Exercises

a. The player stands at the top of the penalty-area retaining arc and faces the nearest goal. The player has a ball at the feet. The ball is played gently forward at a slight angle. The player approaches the ball in an arc. With a long last stride, the nonkicking foot is positioned behind and to the side of the ball, pointing toward the intended target. The kicking foot swings back from the hip. With a long straight leg swing, the player strikes the ball below the midline with the instep. In one fluid motion, the player follows through the middle of the ball and up to loft the ball over the cross bar. The technique is repeated from the other side of the goal. (See Figures 7–9 a and b.) Time used: six minutes.

b. Ten field players and a goalkeeper practice together. One group of five players stands at the top right corner of the penalty-area. The other group stands at the top left corner of the penalty-area. The goalkeeper stands in the center circle. A player from one of the groups pushes the ball two to three yards forward and executes a lofted pass toward the goalkeeper. If the goalkeeper catches the ball before it bounces within the center circle, a goal is scored. A player from the other group now attempts to score. The group with the highest number of successful completions is the winner. Distance may be modified to suit players. Time used: twelve minutes.

c. Ten players are divided into a group of six and a group of four. The group of six players plays three versus three keep-away soccer in the penalty-area. The group of four players (two strikers and two back players) plays keep-away soccer in the center circle. On the coach's whistle, the player in the penalty-area who has possession or is receiving the ball executes a lofted pass into the wing area. At the same time, the striker

Figure 7–9a. Lofted pass. *Note:* Side on approach of the player.

Figure 7–9b. *Note:* Inside of supporting foot is placed just back and to the side of the ball. The striking foot sweeps through and up with the player's body weight leaning back from the ball so as to cause the ball to rise.

nearest the ball's destination moves quickly to control the ball. The striker is pressured by a defender. The striker may turn, dribble, or pass with the supporting striker in order to shoot on goal. The defending players work hard to win the ball back and prevent a goal from being scored. After every breakdown or goal, practice is restarted with players in different positions. Time used: twenty minutes.

Chip Pass

When properly executed, the chipped pass causes the ball to rise steeply over a short distance and hold its altitude. The chipped pass is most effective in heavy traffic or in a free-kick situation in the attacking third of the field, especially when space through and behind the defending team is restricted. In such a situation the lofted pass would be a "high risk" pass, because its power might carry the ball to the goalkeeper or over the goal line. Based on ground conditions and the situation at hand, you can choose between two methods of chipping the ball.

The *full instep* method is most effective when the ball is stationary or when a player is approaching a ball head on as it rolls toward an opponent's goal. Suppose, for example, a defending team has placed a wall of players just outside its penalty-area to prevent a direct free kick on goal. The offensive team, using a set play to combat this move, chooses to chip the ball over the wall of players. The kicker executes a full instep chipped pass over the wall, enabling a supporting player to move onto the ball instead of chasing it.

In order to properly execute the full instep chipped pass, you must take ground condition into consideration. The ground should be soft or thickly coated with grass so that the player's toe can strike the lowest point of the ball with a stabbing action (Figure 7–10). Hit in this manner, the ball will roll up the instep with backspin.

Figure 7–10. Chipping the ball. *Note:* The "full on" approach of the player. Body weight and supporting foot are back from the ball. The striking foot is brought forward sharply, the toes of the foot playing the ball at lowest point causing the ball to rise steeply over a short distance.

The most popular way to chip the ball is with the *inside and top front* of the foot. The player approaches the ball on an arc and strikes it at its lowest point. The player uses a sweeping action similar to that of a golfer chipping a ball out of a sand trap (Figure 7–11). A major advantage of this technique is its versatility. It can be executed on hard, soft, or grassy

Figure 7–11a. Chipping the ball. *Note:* "Side-on" approach of the player. The supporting foot is to the side and slightly back of the ball. The striking foot is open at right angles to the supporting foot.

Figure 7–11b. The striking foot is brought forward, open at right angles to sweep under the ball causing it to rise steeply over 15–25 yards.

ground. Also, the player's forward approach may vary. One disadvantage of this technique is that it is very difficult to impart backspin. Because a sweeping action is used to strike the ball, the contact surface offers little resistance. You might employ this method in a one-on-one situation with a goalkeeper who has left the goal unprotected to close in on you. If you are aware of the goalkeeper's approach, you might try to chip the ball over the goalkeeper's head into the goal.

Common mistakes made when executing the chipped pass include the following:

1. The player's nonkicking foot and body weight are too far behind the ball. This prevents the contact surface from striking the lowest point beneath the ball.

2. The player looks up at the intended target and thus straightens the body. This causes the contact surface to strike the ball just below the midline.

3. The player's leg is too relaxed and follows through the ball.

4. When trying to chip a ball that is rolling away, the player does not move as quickly as the ball.

Practice Exercises

a. The goalkeeper stands on the goal line between the posts, holding a ball. The field player stands at the top of the penalty-area retaining arc, facing the goalkeeper. The goalkeeper rolls the ball toward the field player, moves off the goal line, and stands at the top of the goal area line. The field player approaches the ball head on. The nonkicking foot is close to the front of the ball and points toward the intended target. The kicking leg is raised from the hip, knee bent. The leg swings forward, foot slightly extended, ankle locked. When the knee straightens, the toes strike the ball at the lowest possible point. This lifts the ball up the curve of the instep and high over the goalkeeper's head. Time used: six minutes.

b. The players are divided into teams for a relay competition. They stand behind the touchline, facing infield. The distance between each team along the touchline should be approximately fifteen yards. Two players from each team face their own teams. We will label them players A and B. Player B is ten yards away, with a ball at the feet. Player A stands ten yards behind player B. On the coach's signal, player B side foot passes the ball to the player at the head of the line. This player executes a chipped pass over player B's head so that player A can control the ball. Then, the player at the head of the line replaces player B and player B replaces player A. Player A dribbles the ball around the team and passes it to player B, who restarts the sequence. The first team to restore its original players A and B to the front of the line wins. Time used: twelve minutes.

c. The players are divided into three groups. One group of players stands in the center circle. Each player has a ball at his or her feet. These players are given numbers. The other two groups of players, forwards and backs, line up on either side of the goal posts. These players are paired off, forwards versus backs, and are numbered in the same fashion as the first group. Practice commences with the players in the center circle dribbling around in any direction. The coach calls out an assigned number and the players whose number is called respond immediately. The ball carrier dribbles and passes the ball to a supporting attacker. The supporting attacker should be at or beyond the top of the penalty-area retaining arc and man marked by the defending counterpart. The ball must be controlled and quickly passed back to the original ball carrier, so that he or she can use one of the chipping techniques. The amount of space behind the defending player determines whether the ball should be chipped directly into the goal or chip passed to the supporting player to attempt a goal. Players rotate positions. Time used: thirty minutes.

CHAPTER EIGHT

Shooting with Power and Accuracy Wins Games

The ability to shoot with power and accuracy will be the reward of a player who masters shooting techniques and develops the qualities of intuition, confidence, composure, and determination. Remember, one must score goals to win a game. Teaching the tactical, mechanical aspects of creating goal scoring opportunities can be very frustrating at all levels of the game if no scores result. Maintaining ball possession and playing soccer will be useless if players cannot score when given the chance. Prolific goal scorers are vital to a team's overall success.

The coach's greatest task is to convince one player that another player is more proficient when it comes to scoring goals. Every young player want to experience the thrill of kicking the ball into the opponent's net. Usually, in addition to pressure from opponents, a player who is about to shoot on goal must contend with pressure from supporting players who would like to score the goal themselves. The coach should neither condone this situation nor reprimand the players. A good coach will stress that such a widespread desire for recognition could ruin that particular scoring opportunity or even lose the game.

When teaching shooting techniques, the coach must stress the following points.

1. Today's player must be able to shoot effectively with both feet. This poses a double threat to the defending team.

2. Power and accuracy are equally important. To sacrifice one for the other reduces the player's chances of scoring.

3. All shooting practice must include a goalkeeper. This will help the players learn to judge the best shooting angles.

4. Most shots on goal result from a player's striking a moving ball. The coach should use a moving ball in practice sessions.

5. Every shot on goal must be followed, in anticipation of a rebound.

We can categorize the shooting technique as shots taken when the ball is either stationary or rolling, and shots taken from air balls.

The basic techniques for kicking a rolling or stationary ball are the full instep approach, the instep-side on approach, and swerving the ball (banana shots).

Since power, accuracy, and keeping the ball low are the major aims in all shooting techniques, the principles of execution mentioned in Chapter 6 also apply here. Power is determined by knee action and the foot's speed as it strikes the ball. Once again, the speed of a player's approach and his or her weight distribution influence the shot's effectiveness.

Full Instep

The full instep shot (see Figure 8–1a) is the riskiest shooting technique. This makes it one of the most difficult shots to execute. The player

Figure 8–1a. Full instep shot. *Note:* The ankle of the striking foot is locked down causing the full instep (along the laces) to come in contact with the ball. The supporting foot is placed along the side of the ball and the player's body weight is directly over the ball.

Figure 8–1b. With very little back lift of the striking foot explodes through the ball with a very sharp knee action. The player's head and striking foot are forced down causing the ball to stay low to the ground.

must lock the ankle down so that the instep is held approximately at right angles to the ground. If the player strikes the ball below the midline it is quite possible for the foot to become jammed in the ground. This causes an ankle injury. Proper execution of this technique requires a lot of practice and confidence. This technique is most effective when the player has the widest possible target and approaches the ball and the goal head on.

For example, a striker speedily dribbles the ball toward the goal. The striker is being heavily pressured by an opponent. The nonkicking foot is planted alongside the ball, facing the target. The striker executes a full instep shot on goal.

Practice Exercises

a. The player places a ball about eighteen inches away from the base of a kickboard or similar flat surface. The player takes one step back. The nonkicking foot is beside the ball. The front of the foot should be level with the front of the ball, and the knee should be slightly bent. The leg of the kicking foot is brought back, in line with the middle vertical plane of the ball. The player raises the leg back from the hips, knee slightly bent, ankle locked, instep held approximately at right angles to the ground. The player's body weight is thrown forward. The center of balance and eyes are slightly ahead of the ball. The player may place the hands against the kickboard for support. The player swings the leg forward, tensing all the muscles. Just before impact, the player quickly moves the foot to strike the ball with the full instep, at or just above the midline. The player watches the foot strike and follow through the ball; the player must be able to see if he or she has used proper technique. Time used: five minutes.

b. Two field players (one acting as a goalkeeper) practice together. The goalkeeper stands at the kickboard's midpoint, with his or her back against the board. A duplicate set of target numbers is marked across the bottom fourth of the kickboard. Low numbers are close to the goalkeeper, high numbers are farther away. The other player stands twelve yards away, facing the goalkeeper. This player directly approaches the ball at his or her feet, plants the nonkicking foot alongside it in the intended direction of the shot, and executes a full instep shot at a target number. The players change positions and compete for the most accurate shots. Time used: ten minutes.

c. Four forwards and a goalkeeper practice together. The goalkeeper stands at the kickboard's midpoint, his or her back against the board. One of the forwards stands at a marker located about eighteen yards away from the goalkeeper. This forward has one ball near his or her feet and faces the goalkeeper. Four extra soccer balls are placed close to the marker. On a given signal, the player moves the ball forward (only one touch is allowed) and executes a full instep shot at a target number. As soon as the ball has been played forward, the goalkeeper tries to narrow down the ball's angle toward the target. When possible, the goalkeeper saves the shot. The player, regardless of the eventual outcome of the shot, must race back to the marker, take another ball, and repeat the procedure. The player is given fifteen seconds to shoot all five balls. The player who accumulates the highest number of points in the allotted time wins. Time used: fifteen minutes.

Instep Power Shot

The most popular shooting technique is the instep power shot. This shot is relatively easy to execute, regardless of how a player approaches the ball. Also, there is little danger of the player's hitting the ground when attempting an instep power shot.

The principles of execution of this technique are very similar to those of the instep pass. In this case, however, the player's main aim is to make an accurate powerful shot. When executing the instep pass, the player must also consider the receiver's ability to receive and control the ball.

The instep power kick might be executed in the following situation. A player has the ball under control and is moving toward the goal. Seeing an opportunity to shoot a goal, the player pushes the ball forward and to the side. The player approaches the ball at an angle, plants the nonkicking foot alongside it in the direction of the target, and executes an instep power shot.

Practice Exercises

a. The player stands about twelve yards from a kickboard, with a ball at the feet. The ball is played forward. The player quickly approaches it at an angle. The nonkicking foot is planted beside the ball in the direction of the intended target. The knee is slightly bent, body weight and center of balance are over the ball. The player's kicking foot is extended back, knee slightly bent, foot partially open. The foot is raised and the leg is brought vigorously forward. The foot moves with explosive force from the knee to strike the ball at or just above the midline on a horizontal plane. The player's forward momentum and the speed with which the instep strikes through the ball should force the player's head to almost come into contact with the knee of the kicking foot. The player follows the shot toward the kickboard and controls the rebound. (See Figure 8–2.) Time used: five minutes.

Figure 8–2. Practicing the power instep shot. *Note:* The player's feet leave the ground momentarily after striking the ball. This causes the player's total body weight to be accelerated through the ball for maximum force or power.

Figure 8–3. Practicing for technique, full and power instep shot. Players shoot for accuracy under pressure of time.

b. The players are divided into groups of three. They stand eighteen yards from the kickboard and face it. On a given signal, the first four players (one from each group) play control and shoot soccer for forty-five seconds. Shots must be made with the instep, from no closer than ten yards from the kickboard, and must be aimed at target numbers. The group that gains the highest number of points in the allotted time wins. Several soccer balls should be available to the working group and a time-clock should be used. (See Figure 8–3.) Time used: ten minutes.

c. The players are divided into two groups. Group A is made up of attackers; group B is made up of defenders. Group A players stand behind each other on the halfway line. The group leader has a ball at the feet. Group B players sit behind each other on the halfway line about five yards away from group A. Both groups face the goalkeeper. On a given signal, a player from group A dribbles the ball toward the goalkeeper. The moment the ball is played, a defending player from group B chases the player with the ball, exerting heavy pressure. The player with the ball, while adjusting to being pressured by the defending player, executes an instep power shot from the edge of the penalty-area. The goalkeeper cannot leave the goal area. Groups alternate attacking and defending positions. The group that scores the highest number of goals wins. Time used: fifteen minutes.

The Banana Shot

The banana shot, or "swerving the ball," is another soccer technique introduced by the South American countries. The banana shot may be executed with the inside or outside of the foot. With this shot, the player's ability to powerfully and accurately "bend" the ball, regardless of how it approaches the goal, is devastating. The technique developed from the almost natural curve that players impart to the ball when crossing an air ball, especially from corner kicks. Teams that take advantage of defensive heading and goalkeeping weaknesses often have both wingers cross the ball from opposite corner flags and swerve the ball under the cross bar.

The development of the banana shot, has given an added dimension to the offensive threat of the "one-footed" player. The principles applied to executing the banana shot are similar to those introduced in connection with the instep power shot and the lofted pass. There is, however, one major difference. When one is using this technique, the ball is hit vertically on its left or right side. If the player strikes the ball on its right side, it will spin toward the left, and vice versa.

When should one use the banana shot? One perfect situation follows. The defending team has committed an offense just outside of their own penalty-area. This has given the attacking team a direct free kick. The defending team sets up a wall of four players to protect two-thirds of the goal. The goalkeeper is positioned in view of the ball and protects the remaining third of the goal. An attacking player plays the ball laterally to a supporting attacker. The supporting attacker executes a banana shot that swerves around the wall of defending players toward the goalkeeper. The ball swerves away from the goalkeeper and into the goal. Proper execution of the banana shot is very difficult. It takes many practice sessions to perfect it.

To teach your players how to use the banana shot, follow the guidelines given for teaching the instep power shot and the lofted pass. Remember to stress that the ball is hit vertically on its left or right side.

Practice Exercises

   a. The player stands twelve yards from a kickboard, with a ball at the feet. The ball is played gently forward toward the left side of the kickboard. The player approaches the ball and directly faces the intended target. The nonkicking foot is beside the ball, far enough away to allow the striking foot to hit the ball on its left side (see Figure 8–4). The ball spins and bends from left to right into the target number. The player repeats the technique with the outside of the left foot, approaching the ball from the opposite direction. Time used: six minutes.

   b. The players are divided into groups A and B. They stand in the opposite top corners of the penalty-area, facing the nearest goal. Each group A player has a ball at the feet. On a given signal, the first player dribbles the ball three to five yards along the top of the penalty-area toward group B, and then passes it with the inside of the foot toward the penalty

Figure 8–4. Banana shot, bending or swerving the ball when it is struck with the outside of the foot. *Note:* The ankle is locked down and in towards supporting foot. This causes the ball to swerve from left to right when it is struck.

Figure 8–5. Banana shot, bending or swerving the ball when it is struck with the inside of the foot. *Note:* The ankle is locked down and with the foot open. This causes the ball to swerve from right to left when it is struck. See Figure 7–9 and Figure 8–1 for the mechanics of lifting and keeping the ball low.

spot. As soon as the ball has been passed, a player from group B approaches the ball, full faces the intended target (the far post), and plants the nonkicking foot beside the ball. The player diagonally kicks the ball on its right (see Figure 8–5), driving it in the opposite direction. The ball will spin and bend inside of the far post. Players then change groups. Time used: twelve minutes.

c. Players A, B, C, and a goalkeeper practice together. Player A stands ten yards beyond the top corner of the penalty-area, facing the nearest goal (toward the center line), with a ball at the feet. Player C stands directly across the field in line with player A. Player B stands on the penalty spot, facing infield. Player A air or ground passes the ball to player B. Player B passes it to player C. The moment player B passes the ball, player C executes a banana shot with either the inside of the right foot or the outside of the left foot. Proper execution of the technique will cause the ball to spin and bend in the direction of the far post. Players then change positions. Time used: fifteen minutes.

These three sample practices may also be utilized by the coach to teach the high swerving shot. The mechanics are identical, except that the area of impact is below the ball's midline.

Full and Side Volley Shots

Air balls are usually volley kicked because the kicker lacks time and space in the congested area of the goal. The volley kick or pass can also be very effective outside of the goal area. Many scoring opportunities are missed because players choose to control the ball first. This gives defending players enough time to close in, and the goalkeeper time to reposition and prepare for any shot made on goal. The player who masters the art of volley shooting will be a constant threat to opponents, catching them by surprise with this shot. For example, a corner kick can be lofted over central covering defenders to an attacker on the blind side of the defense. The attacker then executes a full instep volley shot, driving the ball back toward the far post. (See Figures 8–6 and 8–7.) Volley shooting, particularly on goal, requires perfect timing, touch, and extreme confidence.

Figure 8–6. Full instep volley. *Note:* The position of the striking foot. The ankle is locked down causing the ball to make contact along the laces. The knee is high, the head forced down and the ball is struck with a short snappy knee action, with little follow through. This technique is preferred when the player's time and space is restricted.

Figure 8–7. The side foot volley. *Note:* The player moves directly behind the flight of the ball and then opens up the striking foot to make contact on or above the midline of the ball. This technique is preferred when the player is afforded time and space since a greater contact surface ensures greater accuracy.

Common mistakes made when executing the full or side volley are as follows.

1. The player fails to move into line with the flight of the ball.
2. The player kicks under the ball rather than through the midline.
3. The player fails to lean away from the ball and thus restricts full leg and body swing.
4. The player fails to lock and extend the ankle.

Practice Exercises

a. The player stands two yards away from, and facing, the kickboard, holding a ball. The player underhand pitches the ball at a target about three feet above the kickboard's base. As soon as the ball rebounds from the board, the player moves directly in front of the ball's line of flight. Just before the ball hits the ground, the player executes a full instep volley shot back against the board. The player moves his or her foot horizontally. leans away from the ball, and propels it low into the board. Time used: five minutes.

b. The players are divided into teams for a relay competition. The teams stand on the top of the goal area box, facing the goal. The players line up behind one another. One player from each team stands on the goal line, holding a ball and facing his or her team. On a given signal, this player underhand pitches the ball to the player at the head of the line.

According to the service of the ball, the receiver may choose either to immediately full instep volley it or to allow it to bounce once. The player executes a full instep volley kick back to the server. The server catches the ball, places it on the goal line, tags the player at the head of the line, and races to the back of the line. The technique is repeated. Time used: ten minutes.

c. Players A, B, C, and a goalkeeper practice together. Player A stands at the penalty spot, holding a ball and facing the goal. Players B and C are at the opposite top corners of the goal area, standing side-in to the goal. Player A serves a regular throw-in, which player B head passes to player C. Player C pivots on the supporting leg, swings the kicking leg in an arching horizontal plane through the ball, and volley kicks the ball at or above the midline (Figure 8–8). Player A then serves to player B, and the players change positions. Time used: twelve minutes.

d. Ten field players and a goalkeeper practice together. Three players stand at one corner flag, with balls at their feet. Three players stand at the opposite corner flag. Two attacking players stand sideways, facing the players with the ball. One attacker stands at the penalty spot. The other attacker stands at the top far corner of the goal area. Two players are defenders and stand inside of the goal posts. One player crosses a ball into the penalty-area toward one of the attackers. According to the service, the receiver will either vertically volley kick the ball back to the opposite corner of the goal, or horizontally kick the ball into the goal. All players take turns being strikers. Time used: twenty minutes.

Figure 8–8. Practicing the full instep volley shot. *Note:* The player moves directly behind the flight of the ball. Then at the right moment he pivots on the supporting foot to pull the ball across the body and to shoot at the intended target. See Figure 8–6 for body mechanics.

Overhead Bicycle Kick

One of the most spectacular shots on goal is the overhead scissor kick. This technique was perfected by one of the world's greatest soccer players, Pelé. In my opinion, the overhead scissor kick has been a major factor in selling the game to our young players and motivating them to play. In fact, many players have been so enthralled with this spectacular, daring technique that they have insisted on using it despite any risks involved. The overhead scissor kick has been attempted by players from all areas of the field, whether it was appropriate or not. Players have even been penalized in some cases for dangerous play, because their opponents were in danger of being kicked.

Injuries have been caused by improper execution of the overhead scissor kick. We all hate to see trainers, coaches, and parents rush onto the field to revive an injured player. After attempting the overhead kick, a player must break his or her fall. The player who fails to break a fall will crash land on the back or neck. Therefore, it should be impressed upon the players that situations demanding use of the overhead shot are very rare indeed. When the situation does present itself, players must be totally aware, confident, and careful. A typical situation that might call for use of the overhead shot follows. An arced head or chipped pass is traveling into an attacker who is turned away from the opponent's goal. The player leans back and executes an overhead shot on goal. (See Figure 8–9.)

Figure 8–9. The bicycle kick. *Note:* The player's body leaves the ground momentarily and ball is struck along the instep with a short snappy knee action. The player's hands drop back to cushion the fall.

Practice Exercises

a. The player sits, knees slightly bent, with the back toward a kickboard. The player should be about three yards from the board. The player gently tosses a ball into the air, just above head height. The player leans fully backwards, with the hands in a supporting position on the ground. Both feet are thrown into the air. The kicking leg is slightly bent, the ankle locks, and the toes point outward. With a full leg swing from the hips, the full instep makes contact with the ball and drives it against the kickboard. Following through the shot causes the player's body to rock back and forth. Time used: five minutes.

b. Players are divided into teams for a relay competition. The players on each team sit behind one another behind the goal line. The teams are five yards apart. A team captain kneels in front of his or her team, facing the team. The captain is six yards away from the team. A second player from the team sits facing the team captain, halfway between the captain and the player at the head of the line. On a given signal, the team captain underhand pitches the ball just above head height to the sitting player. The player overhead kicks the ball to the next player in line. This player must catch or retrieve the ball. The team captain races to the back of the line. The captain is replaced by the kicker, and the kicker is replaced by the retriever. The first team to have all their players back in their original positions wins. Time used: ten minutes.

c. Players, A, B, and C (one acts as a goalkeeper) practice together. Player A stands in the penalty-area retaining arc, facing the goal. Player B, the ball holder, stands at the penalty spot and faces player A. Player C is the goalkeeper. Player B serves an underhand pitch into the air, which player A heads back into the penalty-area. Once the ball is in the penalty-area, player B executes an overhead shot on the goalkeeper, player C. All players take turns practicing the technique. Time used: ten minutes.

CHAPTER NINE

Dribbling: A Natural Talent

There are many ways of penetrating the opposing team's defense. (See chapter six.) From time to time, however, defensive organization will dominate the play to such an extent that penetration and shots on goal are restricted to a minimum. Soccer has become more organized with a variety of systems of play. Because of the modern player's knowledge and well-rounded playing skill, we even see playing systems change during the course of a game to overcome an opponent's strengths or take advantage of weaknesses. Such an emphasis on organization may lead the observer to find soccer an unattractive game that restricts the player's individuality. The coach, on the contrary, knows that the game needs strong, unique players. Creative, spontaneous players can turn a well-organized defense into total confusion and chaos.

Dribbling appears to be an innate talent found in all young novice players. Although they may be somewhat lacking in direction and lateral mobility, the coach has a firm foundation from which to nurture these talents.

The basic principles of dribbling are as follows:

1. The player must concentrate on keeping the ball within playing distance and away from the opponent.

2. The player should be perfectly balanced so that he or she can move in any direction when challenged by an opponent.

3. The player should, by using a series of feet and upper body movements, try to laterally move the opponent into an off-balance position.

4. The player should display change of pace, speed off the mark, and accelerate away from an opponent.

Common dribbling mistakes are as follows:

1. The player fails to look up from the ball and loses his or her sense of direction and awareness of surroundings.
2. The player's touch or feel for the ball is too heavy. This causes the player to push the ball too far ahead and lose control.
3. If the player's body is too straight and stiff, lateral mobility is restricted. This often causes the player to run into an opponent.

The three basic dribbling techniques are the inside of the foot technique, the outside of the foot technique, and the front of the foot technique (also known as speed dribbling).

Dribbling, Feinting, and Dodging

The coach must incorporate the three basic dribbling techniques, as well as feinting and dodging, into the training session. All are part and parcel of the player's dribbling skill.

A player's dribbling skills might be evident in the following situation. A winger approaches an opposing wing fullback positioned near the halfway line and close to the touchline. In order to create space down the touchline in which to dribble the ball at speed, the winger dribbles the ball toward the defender. At a comfortable distance, the winger drops the innermost shoulder and the nonplaying foot infield and crouches forward over the ball in an attempt to move the wing fullback into an off-balance position. Once the wing fullback is committed to this feint, the winger slides the playing foot across and behind the ball. He or she plays it with the outside of the foot, pushing off from the nonplaying foot to accelerate past the wing fullback. (See Figure 9–1.)

Practice Exercises

a. All players stand around the center circle. On the coach's command, all the players slowly dribble their balls in the same direction around the circle. With the inside of the left and the right foot they play the balls back and forth across the center circle line. The players' upper bodies must be inclined slightly forward, eyes on the ball when making contact, and ankles relaxed. The players reverse direction on command. Continuous touching of the ball with the feet should be encouraged by the coach. Time used: three minutes.

Figure 9–1a. Dribbling, the Stanley Matthews feint. *Note:* The dipping of the left shoulder and the bending of the left leg. The playing foot is raised as if to pull the ball across the opponent.

Figure 9–1b. The foot sweeps past and behind the ball causing the opponent to turn inside. At this moment the player pushes the ball with the outside of the foot in the opposite direction and into the space created.

      b. All players stand around the center circle, an equal distance apart. The players are assigned numbers. On the coach's command, they slowly dribble the balls in the same direction around the circle, using the inside and outside of the foot. The coach calls out two of the assigned numbers. The players whose numbers are called must turn and dribble the ball in the opposite direction, dodging and weaving through the other players who are still dribbling slowly around the outside of the center circle. When the two players return to their original positions, the coach calls out another two numbers. The exercise continues until all players have completed the task. The coach can also introduce tag into this drill. The tagger must be in control of the ball. Time used: six minutes.

c. All players stand in a twenty-by-twenty-yard grid or in the center circle, with balls at the feet. The coach then assigns the following reactions to various hand signals made above the head. One finger up on the right hand means dribble the ball with the inside of both feet (one touch only) clockwise in the training area. One finger up on the left hand means dribble counterclockwise; two fingers up means dribble the ball with the outside of the feet; three fingers up means dribble the ball with the inside and outside of one foot only; four fingers up means stop the ball using any part of the foot. The players feint as if to dribble in one direction, only to slide the playing foot across and behind the ball to play it with the outside of the foot in the opposite direction. The practice commences on the coach's signal. (See Figure 9–2.) Time used: six minutes.

d. Player A stands on the touchline, facing infield with a ball at the feet. Player B stands facing player A approximately five yards away. Player B jogs backwards across the field. The moment player B moves, player A dribbles the ball toward player B, using the inside and outside of the foot. Player B, at any given time, may stop and make as if to challenge for the ball. At this moment, player A must play the ball to the side, using either the inside or outside of the foot, in order to dodge player B. Player A then controls and dribbles the ball at speed about five yards beyond player B. Player A then passes the ball to player B, who will now dribble the ball toward player A. This continues from touchline to touchline. Time used: six minutes.

Figure 9–2. Practicing for technique all types of dribbling and touch and look up soccer.

e. Six players play three-aside soccer in a thirty-by-twenty-yard grid. The team in possession of the ball may play regular soccer in its defending half of the grid. However, once the ball has been passed or dribbled into the opponent's half, the player receiving the pass or dribbling the ball must beat one opponent before a goal can be scored or before regular soccer can be resumed. Should the team in possession of the ball lose it in its own defending half, the new ball carrier must beat one opponent before a goal can be scored or before regular soccer can be resumed. Time used: ten minutes. Note: Goals are set one yard apart. Only two attackers may enter the opponent's half of the grid. The third player will be the sweeper back.

Speed Dribbling with a Change of Pace

Many wingers who lack the guile to feint and dodge past their opponents base their escape on speed off the mark, the ability to change pace, and exceptional ball control. Speed dribbling might be "on" in the course of a game in either of the following situations.

In the first situation, the winger receives the ball from a supporting player and catches the opposing wing fullback in a deep supporting position. The winger quickly takes advantage of the open space by attacking at speed (using a lengthy stride). The winger touches the ball just below

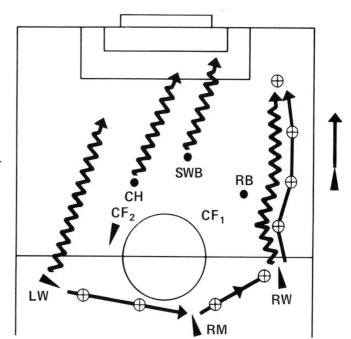

Figure 9–3. Functional training for technique "speed dribbling" through the wing area.

the midline in a central, vertical plane. The winger moves directly and challenges the wing fullback to make the first move. At the right moment, the winger touches the ball wide and dodges the wing fullback. The winger then changes pace to a short, powerful, piston-like leg action, accelerating toward goal or down the wing to cross the ball. (See Figure 9–3.)

Here is the second situation. After making a save, the goalkeeper punts the ball in the direction of the lead striker. The striker lays a pass back to a supporting midfielder. The defending players anticipate a pass to the attacking forwards, who move into supporting positions. The defending players are quickly closed down. The midfielder takes advantage of the width that has been gained by supporting forwards by attacking

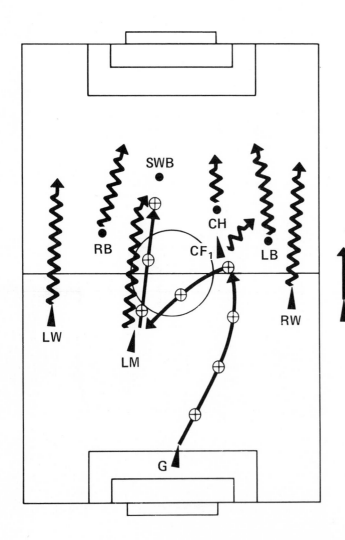

Figure 9–4. Functional training for technique "speed dribbling" attacking central space.

this space and the defending sweeperback. At the right moment, the midfielder touches the ball wide, dodges, accelerates, and speed dribbles toward the opponent's goal for a shot. (See Figure 9–4.)

Practice Exercises

a. Player A and player B each stand at a goal post and face the nearest corner flag. Both have balls. On a given signal, both players speed dribble along the goal line. They touch the ball with the front of the foot, using a long stride. When both players reach the intersection of the goal line and the penalty-area line, they stop the balls with their feet and turn infield. After a short rest (about seven seconds), both players dribble at speed along the outer penalty-area lines. They use short, choppy leg action. At the top corners of the penalty-area they stop the ball. Both players rest for another seven seconds. Then, they face each other. On a given signal, the players speed dribble toward each other along the length of the penalty-area line, using a long stride. As soon as they pass each other, the players must change pace and use short choppy strides until they reach the corners of the penalty-area. Players A and B continue to dribble the ball at a relaxed pace around the perimeter of the penalty-area and back to their goal post. Each player makes three complete circuits. Time used: five minutes.

b. The players are divided into two groups, forwards and backs. The teams stand at the top of the penalty-area, with players behind one another and in line with the goal posts. The player at the head of each line has a ball at the feet. On a given signal, both players speed dribble, using short choppy strides, around their respective goal posts. Once around the goal

Figure 9–5. Team relays to improve individual player technique. The player strikes the ball along the laces, plays the ball along a straight line. "Touch and look up soccer."

post, the players speed dribble back to their line, changing their pace to a long stride. The ball is passed to the next player, and the technique is repeated by each player. (See Figure 9–5.) Time used: six minutes.

c. The players are again divided into two groups, forwards and backs. The teams sit down behind the goal line, facing the outer penalty-area lines on either side of the goal post. The players at the head of line have a ball at the feet. On a given signal, they jump up and speed dribble the ball diagonally across the penalty-area toward the penalty-area retaining arc. At the intersection of the penalty-area line and the retaining arc, the players change pace. They dribble the ball around the arc, dodge each other, and change pace once again. This time, they speed dribble diagonally back across the penalty-area. The ball is passed to the next player in line, who repeats the technique. (See Figure 9–6.) The teams change positions. Time used: nine minutes.

d. The players are divided into four teams, two of forwards and two of backs. The players in each team are assigned numbers beginning with one. The two defending teams stand near the goals at opposite ends of the field. Each player holds a ball. The two attacking teams stand in the center circle and face their respective defensive teams. Play commences when the coach calls out one of the assigned numbers. The four players whose numbers are called must react immediately. The defenders volley kick the ball in the direction of the center circle and then sprint out beyond the penalty-area. The moment the ball is kicked, the attackers move quickly to control and speed dribble the ball toward their respective defenders. At the right moment, the attackers will play the ball off to the side, dodge the defenders, and shoot on goal. Players rotate. Time used: ten minutes. Note: The defenders must not retreat beyond the top of the penalty-area. In the event of a breakdown in play, the coach will call another number. All teams take turns being attackers.

Screening the Ball

All players must know how to maintain ball possession while under an opponent's extreme pressure. To maintain possession in tight situations, the player must be able to screen the ball. This is done by placing the body between the ball and an opponent, while staying within playing distance of the ball. Wingers must be particularly adept at screening the ball, as they are often restricted near touchlines or corners of the field by intelligent opponents. For example, suppose a winger had been pressured into an attacking corner of the field by an opposing wing fullback. The winger might decide to hold and screen the ball until a supporting player was within passing range. The winger would turn sideways to the wing fullback, lean one shoulder slightly toward the opponent, and play the ball with the opposite foot; that is, left shoulder–right foot (see Figure 9–6).

Figure 9–6. Screening the ball. *Note:* The player with the ball is side on to the opponent and the leg of the playing foot fully extended. The outside of the foot plays the ball.

Practice Exercises

a. Two players practice together in a ten-by-ten-yard grid. One player plays keep-away ball by using good screening tactics. The other player offers only limited pressure. Players change positions after thirty-five seconds. Time used: three minutes.

b. Players A and B practice together in a twenty-by-ten-yard grid. Player A stands on one grid line with a ball at the feet. Player B stands twenty yards away, facing player A. Play commences when player A dribbles the ball and tries to hold it on the halfway grid line with the foot to score two goals. Player B must prevent the goals from being scored and attempt to win the ball. Player A also has the choice of screening the ball for fifteen seconds to score one goal. Time used: six minutes. Note: Players alternate positions after each goal or breakdown.

c. Players A, B, and C practice together. Player A stands at the corner flag with a ball at the feet. Player B stands at the intersection of the goal line and the penalty-area line. Player C stands at the goal post nearest player B. Play commences when player A passes the ball to player B, who is immediately pressured by player C. With good screening, player B must try to hold the ball until player A is in the penalty-area. Then, with good feinting and dribbling, player B must try to get the ball to player A for a shot on goal. All players alternate positions. Time used: ten minutes. Note: Player B must not enter the penalty-area. A goalkeeper may be used.

CHAPTER TEN

Heading

Major sports in the United States revolve around using the hands. Athletes throw, catch, pass, and dribble with their hands. In soccer, the use of the hands is restricted to the goalkeeper and restart situations. The fact that the game encourages total body use is seen by many as amazing and bewildering. Even more astonishing is the frequent use of the head to propel the ball. Although modern-day coaching emphasizes basic soccer, or keeping the ball on the ground, making a high cross from the wings for a head shot on goal is still a sound tactical move. Weaknesses in goalkeeping and defensive heading can be exploited to the fullest. Thus heading techniques are vital ingredients of the game.

Since heading the ball is regarded by most of our young players as a novelty that requires a certain amount of courage, the teaching of heading techniques is usually met with enthusiasm. Most young or novice players quickly gain confidence in their ability to master the art of heading, unless they have had an earlier painful experience. The coach must be patient and understanding. A careful progressive program of technical development should be presented.

During the course of a game, the player may be required to head the ball when both feet are firmly on the ground, or when both feet are off the ground.

When the player is on the ground, the following points must be stressed.

1. When heading for accuracy, the player must play the ball on the front of the forehead.

2. When heading for power and accuracy, the player must be sure

the feet are astride at the moment of contact. This will provide balance and maximize trunk movement.

3. The player must attack the ball by throwing the eyes and head toward and through the ball to the intended target.

4. When heading the ball off to the side, the player must turn the head so that contact is made with the forehead.

5. If the situation demands that the ball be headed high into the air, the player must strike the ball below its midline and push up and through it on a vertical plane. If the player is aiming at a supporting player's feet, he or she should strike the ball above its midline and push down and through it on a vertical plane.

6. The decision to head the ball must be made early, so that the trunk and head can be cocked in order to fire the ball in the intended direction.

If the player must jump to head the ball, all the above principles will apply, except number two. The coach should stress the following points for proper execution.

1. To reach maximum height, use the one-footed technique. This is the way platform divers gain the height they need to execute tumbles, twists, or jackknives. The stride onto the take-off foot should be long, with the player leaning slightly back. As the take-off foot strikes the ground, the player pushes up powerfully, using the arms to assist the upward momentum. Both legs are vigorously brought forward as if for a jackknife. This adds to the body's upward thrust and to the head's forward thrust. (See Figure 10–1.)

2. When the player does not have the space to run and jump, the two-footed take-off is usually preferred. To gain maximum height, the player bends slightly at the knees. The body is then thrust vertically into the air. The player uses his or her arms to assist the upward movement. The trunk and head are cocked back, allowing for maximum power through the ball. The legs are lifted back and up so the shins are parallel to the ground. Proper execution causes the player to hang in the air. (See Figure 10–2.)

Heading for Height and Distance

Heading for height and distance out of a congested penalty-area takes timing and courage. A timely clearance avoids panic, keeps goals from being scored, and provides time for the defending team to regroup. Heading for height and distance would be appropriate, for example, from a corner kick. A high ball crosses into the penalty-area, toward the penalty

Figure 10–1. Heading for height and distance. *Note:* The player uses a one footed vertical hop for gaining maximum body lift. The forehead strikes below the mid-line of the ball and the head and trunk are brought vigorously forward, forming a jackknife.

Figure 10–2. Heading for height, distance and head shots on goal. *Note:* This technique is preferred when the player's time and space is restricted. *Note:* Also, the players use a two footed vertical jump and draw the legs back to gain space. See Figure 10–1 for comparison of technique.

spot. A defending player decides to head the ball. This player propels the ball high and wide toward the touchline.

Practice Exercises

a. The player holds the ball in the hands, arms extended upward at a forty-five-degree angle. The player brings the ball down to strike the front of the forehead, and then repeats the action for feel and confidence. Time used: one minute.

b. Players A and B kneel three yards apart, facing each other. Player A underhand throws the ball so that player B can head it. As soon as the ball is released, player B rocks backward on his or her heels and sets the trunk and head for proper execution. Player B then fires the trunk and head forward and pulls on two imaginary posts with the hands. This pulling action helps the player to gather the momentum needed to head the ball back to player A. Players A and B take turns executing this technique. Time used: three minutes.

c. Player A stands on the middle of the goal line. Player B, the ball carrier, stands on the goal area line and faces player A. Player C stands on the penalty spot, facing and directly in line with players A and B. Practice begins when player B throws the ball toward player A. The ball should travel half the distance between players A and B. Player A approaches the ball, makes a one-footed vertical take-off, cocks the trunk and neck, and snaps the head up through the ball to propel it to player C. Player A sprints six yards past player C. The practice is then repeated: player C becomes the new server, and the players move down the length of the field. Time used: six minutes. Note: This could also be used as a relay competition.

d. Eight players practice together. Six players stand on the sides of the penalty-area, three on each side. All the players hold balls. An attacking player stands at the penalty spot. One other player stands at the top of the goal area box. One of the players with a ball volley kicks it in the direction of the attacker. As soon as the ball has been kicked, the defending player approaches it and heads the ball out of the penalty-area. The attacker offers only passive resistance. The services come alternately from the two sides of the penalty-area. All players receive six serves. Time used: twenty minutes.

Heading for Power and Direction
(Head Shots on Goal)

Heading for shots on goal, whether the player's feet are on the ground or in the air, requires skill, timing, and courage. The attacking

Figure 10–3. Head shot on goal. *Note:* How the player's time and space is restricted. The two footed vertical jump in this instance is preferred. The player's forehead is above/over the ball so as to propel it down into the goal.

player is often under heavy pressure from defending players. The player must strike the ball with the front of the forehead above its midline in order to direct it into the goal or near a supporting player. A head shot on goal might be used after a well-hit cross from a winger lands in the penalty area. A supporting attacker, seeing the opportunity for a head shot on goal, moves quickly into the ball's line of flight and strikes it with the forehead above the midline, sending it down into the goal. (See Figure 10–3.)

Practice Exercises

   a. The player suspends a tether ball from the cross bar so that the eyes are level with the midline of the ball. The player then stands on his or her toes and leans back from the hips. The arms are brought up as if holding an imaginary post. The trunk and head are cocked and then fired forward. The front of the forehead makes contact with the ball above its midline. The arms are pulled back in toward the chest to provide momentum. The player maintains the original position and repeatedly heads the ball. (See Figure 10–5.) Time used: three minutes.

   b. The players are divided into teams for a relay competition. The teams stand along the touchline, players behind one another. Team captains face their respective teams from about five yards away. On a given signal, each team captain throws the ball at about head height toward the player at the head of the line. The moment the ball has been released, the receiver steps forward to meet it. The receiver leans back, cocks the trunk and head, and strikes the ball above its midline. The head follows through, propelling the ball back and down to the team captain's feet. The team captain controls the ball and then is replaced by the player at the head of the line. The team captain races to the back of the line. The first team to restore its captain to the original position wins. Time used: ten minutes.

c. The players are divided into teams according to height. They line up five yards away from each other and face tether balls suspended from the cross bar. Each team's ball is six inches higher than the tallest player on the team. The lead player from each team jogs to the ball and makes a two-footed vertical jump above the ball's midline. The player leans back from the hips and brings the legs back and up to form a number 4. The trunk and head are fired forward to powerfully strike the ball with the front of the forehead. The next player in line repeats the technique. Time used: six minutes.

d. Four players stand across the center line, facing a goalkeeper. Two players act as wingers, and two act as strikers. The goalkeeper volley kicks the ball toward the strikers. One of the strikers controls the ball and then interpasses it with the supporting striker. They move toward the goal. The wingers also move downfield, staying close to the touchline and supporting the strikers. The ball is passed toward one of the corner flags so that one of the wingers can reach it. All other players move into the penalty-area—one to the near post, one near the penalty spot, and one to the far top corner of the goal area. The ball is crossed into the penalty-area so that one of the supporting forwards can either execute a head shot or pass to a supporting player. Wingers must be encouraged to vary the crosses, so that all heading techniques may be attempted. Time used: twenty minutes.

Back Head and Flick Pass

Many goals have been scored with a timely back head or flick pass. When attackers turn their backs to their opponent's goal, or when opponents are caught out of position, it is time to use the back head or flick pass. If these passes are mainly used to surprise an opponent, they will add to a team's potential scoring power. They are very difficult to execute because precise timing and a developed feel for the ball are needed. However, young players should be encouraged to devote some time to practicing these sophisticated techniques.

To properly teach these techniques, the coach must stress the following points.

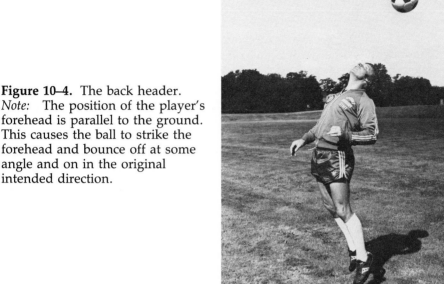

Figure 10–4. The back header.
Note: The position of the player's forehead is parallel to the ground. This causes the ball to strike the forehead and bounce off at some angle and on in the original intended direction.

1. When one is back heading the ball, the head is tilted backwards so that the ball strikes the forehead at the hair line. The ball may either glance off or be pushed up and backwards of the player, depending on the circumstances.

2. To flick head the ball, the head is moved outside of the line of flight of the ball immediately before contact. The ball may glance off, or the head may be twisted to flick the ball away with the side of the forehead.

Practice Exercises

a. A player stands five yards away from a kickboard, holding a ball. The player makes a regular throw-in, aiming for a high spot on the board. On the rebound, the player moves under the ball. Right before contact, the player tilts the head backwards, pushes up through the ball, and propels it on its original path. The player repeats the technique, varying the height of the throw-in against the kickboard. Time used: five minutes.

b. Holding a ball in the hands, player A stands on the touchline and faces the field. Player B stands five yards away, facing player A. Player C stands five yards beyond player B, in a direct line with both other players. Player A makes a regular throw-in on a horizontal plane in the direction of player B. Player B tilts the head backwards and under the ball, allowing the ball to glance off in the direction of player C. The technique is continued, with all players alternating positions. Time used: twelve minutes.

c. The players are divided into teams for a relay competition. Behind the touchline, the players line up behind one another. There should be about two yards between players. Team captains stand five yards in front of their respective teams, facing the team. On a given signal, each team captain throws the ball toward the first player in line. The player moves under the ball and executes a back header to the next player in line. The next player repeats the technique. The ball is propelled backwards until it reaches the last player. This player catches the ball, races to the front of the line, and replaces the team captain. The first team to get the captain back in the original position is the winner. Time used: twelve minutes.

d. Field players A, B, and C and a goalkeeper practice together. Player A stands at the top of the penalty-area retaining arc, centered toward the goal, with a ball in the hands. Player B stands on the retaining arc, an equal distance from player A and the penalty-area line. Player C stands on the penalty-area line facing player A, who is four yards away. Player A throws the ball horizontally at about head height to player C. Player C moves the head outside the line of flight of the ball and executes a head flick pass to player B. Player B takes a first-time shot at the goalkeeper. All players practice the technique. They must be encouraged to use both sides of the forehead. Time used: ten minutes.

e. Five field players practice together in a twenty-by-twenty-yard grid. Four of the players form a diamond using the grid marking. One of these players holds the ball. The fifth player stands in the center of the grid, facing the player with the ball. The player with the ball makes a regular throw-in to the player in the center of the grid. The moment the ball is released, the player standing at the top of the diamond assumes the role of a defender and begins to exert heavy pressure on the receiver. According to the service and the pressure applied by the defending player, the receiver executes either a back header or a head flick pass to one of the supporting players in the wing areas. Playing four on one, the players try to complete ten consecutive one-touch passes. The players then change positions. Time used: ten minutes. (See Figure 10–5.)

f. The players are divided into three groups—right wingers, left wingers, and strikers. The right and left wingers stand near their appropriate corner flag with balls at their feet. The strikers position themselves near the perimeter of the goal area. One of the strikers functions as a target. This player always stands two to three yards beyond the near post, close to the goal line. A player from the right corner flag crosses the ball toward the target person. According to the service of the ball, the striker

Figure 10–5. The head flick pass. Utilizing the grid to improve player technique #1. *Note:* The player moves directly behind the flight of the ball and at the right moment moves the head outside of the flight of the ball, twists upper body and propels the ball with a quick flick of the head to the intended target.

executes either a back header or a head flick, so that a supporting player can shoot on goal. Defenders may be introduced into this practice, including a goalkeeper. Wingers should be encouraged to vary their crosses to include high, hard, low, and inswinger passes. Time used: thirty minutes.

Diving Header

There are many ways to score goals during the course of a game, but none is more spectacular than the diving header. Here, the player throws the body horizontally through the air in order to head the ball, which cannot be reached with any other part of the body. The opportunity to use the diving header often presents itself in congested goal area situations that demand total awareness, perfect timing, daring, and courage.

Like the overhead scissor kick, the diving header is a very risky technique. It is always possible to sustain an injury from an errant kick or an improper landing; it happens even to experienced players. Young novice players must therefore be discouraged from executing this technique in game play until a thorough understanding of the technique has been ac-

Figure 10–6. The diving header. *Note:* The player has thrust the body forward to attack the ball. The body is parallel to the ground. The hands are held ready to support the body and the eyes are "thrown" at the ball.

quired. However, young and old players respond with enthusiasm to a chance to practice diving headers. Diving headers are thus ideal for rounding out a practice session.

The diving header might be used in a match if a hard low cross from one of the wings reached across the face of the goal. A supporting attacking player on the defense's blind side would run, make a single-footed take-off, dive horizontally through the air, and head the ball on target. (See Figure 10–6.)

Practice Exercises

   a. Player A stands and holds a ball. Player B crouches three yards away from and facing player A. Player A gently underhand throws the ball toward player B. Player B thrusts the body forward on a horizontal plane, arms extended, eyes fixed on the ball. Player B strikes the ball with the forehead at or just above the midline, heading it back to player A. The power of the head shot is determined by the speed of player B's forward momentum and snap of the head. Time used: three minutes.

   b. The players are divided into a team of forwards and a team of backs. The teams line up at top far corners of the goal area. They face the goalkeeper, who kneels on the goal line. The team captains stand at the goal post, diagonally opposite their respective teams, with ball in their hands. At a given signal, each team captain throws the ball to the player at the head of the line. The moment the ball has been released, this player moves quickly toward the ball, throws the body horizontally through the air, and propels the ball with the forehead toward the far post. Time used: twenty minutes.

c. Two field players and a goalkeeper practice together in front of a kickboard. The goalkeeper kneels in front of the middle of the kickboard, with a ball in the hands. The two field players crouch down three yards away from and facing the goalkeeper. The players form an equilateral triangle. The goalkeeper throws the ball to one of the players so that he or she can execute a diving header. The moment the ball is released, this player throws the body horizontally through the air to meet the ball. The moment before contact is made, the player twists the body toward the target, turns the head away from the ball, and then twists and snaps the neck and head, power driving the ball toward the target. Time used: six minutes.

d. Players A, B, C, and D stand in the four corners of a ten-by-ten-yard grid. Player A holds a ball in the hands. Players B and C stand adjacent to player A. Player D stands diagonally across from player A.

Figure 10–7. Team relays to improve individual player technique. Diving headers.

Player A throws the ball so that either player B or C can execute a diving header. For example, suppose player A decides to throw the ball to player B. Player B quickly moves toward the ball. According to the service, player B may decide to execute a diving header either back to player A or diagonally across to player C. As soon as player A releases the ball, player D moves into the grid and challenges for possession of the ball. Players A, B, and C now play three on one, attempting to make five consecutive passes. The practice is then restarted by another player. Time used: six minutes.

e. Players A, B, C, and a goalkeeper practice together. The goalkeeper stands on the goal line, facing infield. Player A stands on the penalty spot and faces the goalkeeper. Players B and C stand at the top far corners of the goal area, each one holding a ball. On a given signal, player A moves quickly toward the goal. Player B underhand throws the ball high enough so that player A can execute a diving header from just outside of the goal area. According to the service, player A will make contact with the ball with either the front or the side of the head. Player A immediately jumps up and races back to the penalty spot. Player A then moves quickly toward the goal once again to execute another diving header on a ball thrown underhand by player C. (See Figure 10–7.) Each player attempts to complete as many diving headers on net as possible in thirty-five seconds. The goalkeeper must not leave the goal line. Time used: ten minutes.

CHAPTER ELEVEN

Goalkeepers: The Forgotten Soccer Players

Much time and effort is devoted to developing the players' technical expertise and the team's overall tactical awareness. The goalkeeper, however, receives little training in these vital aspects of the game. This leads me to believe that the goalkeeper is the forgotten soccer player. Too often, the goalkeeper works alone in a secluded corner of the field and is only asked to participate in practice games or shooting exercises. This can frustrate and demoralize the goalkeeper. The position calls for proper technical execution and a sound understanding of the game. The coach must recognize that the goalkeeper is vital to the team's strength and confidence. The coach who devotes time and effort to improving the goalkeeper's basic technique and tactical play will be rewarded.

The basic techniques used to stop the ball are applied by the goalkeeper, except that the goalie can also use the hands. Points to be stressed by the coach follow.

1. The goalkeeper must, whenever possible, move directly in front of the ball's flight.
2. The goalkeeper must, whenever possible, use both hands to catch, punch, or deflect the ball.
3. When stopping a shot on goal, the goalkeeper should let the body or hands "ride" to cushion the impact of the shot.
4. The goalkeeper must concentrate on completing one function at a time. Mistakes are made when the goalkeeper combines more functions, such as catching and throwing the ball or catching the ball and moving at the same time.

5. The goalkeeper must keep the eyes on the player with the ball and on the player off the ball at all times.

Safe hands in all situations, especially in traffic and under challenge, are the hallmark of sound goalkeeping. Once in possession of the ball, the goalkeeper dictates play and becomes the first person in attack. The goalkeeper who hesitates in traffic or under challenge will make many mistakes and lose the rest of the team's respect and confidence.

GATHERING GROUND BALLS

Gathering ground balls is a relatively simple task. Yet many outstanding goalkeepers have been guilty of poorly executing this basic technique. They have found themselves in the embarrassing position of retrieving the ball from the back of the net.

There are two basic techniques for gathering ground balls.

The Standing Technique

To gather low hard shots that pass on the ground or below the knees, most goalkeepers stand erect, legs together, and bend from the waist to gather the ball into their hands. They then cradle the ball against their lower chest (Figure 11–1). There are many practice exercises that will help the goalkeeper improve this technique. The basic ones presented in this chapter can be very beneficial.

Figure 11–1a. Practicing for technique, gathering ground balls.

Figure 11–1b. Cradling the ball for safety. "Goalies ball."

Practice Exercises

a. The goalkeeper kicks the ball against a kickboard and gathers the ball on the rebound.

b. The goalkeeper practices with a partner, who stands about twenty yards away with a ball at the feet. (The partner may also stand on the edge of the penalty-area.) The partner passes or kicks the ball to the goalkeeper, who stops the ball.

c. The goalkeeper practices with a team player, who stands with a ball at the feet on the edge of the penalty-area. The team player passes or kicks the ball to the goalkeeper and then immediately challenges the goalkeeper. The team player hopes to distract the goalkeeper and pounce on any fumble that might be caused by this challenge. This practice can be repeated with variations in the power, height, and pressure of the challenger.

The Kneeling Technique

To gather hard low shots where the goalkeeper must move one or two paces to the left or right, or where conditions are hazardous, the kneeling technique (Figure 11–2) is preferred. The goalkeeper moves directly in front of the ball, feet sideways, the upper torso twisted. The goalkeeper then rests one knee on the ground, and touches the heel of the

Figure 11–2. Practicing for technique gathering ground balls hit to the left or right side of the goalkeeper. *Note:*   Heel of the raised leg touching the knee of the resting or lower leg.

other foot to prevent the ball from slipping through the legs. The goalie uses both hands to gather the ball and cradles it against the lower chest.

Practice Exercises

   a. The goalkeeper places two markers about five yards apart in front of a kickboard. The goalkeeper stands five to eight yards away from the rebound surface, between the two markers. The ball is rolled or kicked toward either marker, and rebounds off the kickboard at an angle. The goalkeeper moves laterally to gather up the ball.

   b. The goalkeeper practices with two partners. One stands ten yards in front of, and the other ten yards behind, the goalkeeper. Both have balls at their feet. The player in front of the goalkeeper side foot passes the ball a few yards to the right. The goalkeeper returns this ball, then turns, receives, and gathers a ball passed in from the left by the other partner.

   c. The goalkeeper practices with six to eight team players. The team players stand around the center circle. The goalkeeper stands in the middle of the circle. The team players pass two soccer balls in any direction around the outside of the circle. The goalkeeper can demand a pass from one of the team players at any time.

   d. The goalkeeper practices with six to eight team players. The team players stand around the center circle. Four markers are placed within the circle, about three yards apart. The markers form a diamond and serve as four goals. The goalkeeper stands in the middle of the diamond, within the circle. One ball is passed around the circle in any direction, until one of the team players sees an opportunity to pass the ball through one of the four goals. The goalkeeper must try to protect all four goals, stopping and gathering the ball whenever possible.

GATHERING HIGH BALLS

Gathering high balls is also a relatively simple task, if the goalkeeper has total concentration. The goalkeeper makes mistakes when under challenge by an opponent, when there is a loss of eye-to-ball concentration, or when there is a crowd of players and movement in the goal area.

The techniques preferred by most goalkeepers for gathering a ball that has been kicked above ground level follow.

Gathering Low Balls

To gather hard shots that travel above the knee and below chest height, the goalkeeper moves directly in front of the ball's flight (Figure 11–3). Goalie's arms should be semiextended and parallel to each other. They form a channel that the ball will roll up. The ball is then cradled against the lower chest, elbows are tucked into the sides, and both hands

Figure 11–3. Practicing for technique gathering an air ball hit above the knee and below chest height. *Note:* Feet are astride for balance.

protect the ball. If the shot is well hit, upon making the save the goalkeeper relaxes the body to absorb the ball's impact.

Practice Exercises

a. The goalkeeper pitches the ball underhand against a kickboard from about two yards away. The ball is thrown high enough so that it rebounds against the goalkeeper's midsection, allowing the goalkeeper to gather it to the chest.

b. The goalkeeper works with a partner who has the ball. The goalkeeper stands about three yards away from the kickboard and faces the partner. As soon as the partner pitches the ball underhand against the kickboard, the goalkeeper pivots and gathers the ball on the rebound. To vary this practice, assign the goalkeeper different positions (i.e., sitting, kneeling) in relation to the rebound surface.

c. The goalkeeper stands on the goal line or touchline and faces his or her partner. The partner stands about ten yards away, holding a ball. The partner underhand pitches the ball toward the goalkeeper. The goalkeeper gathers the ball and returns it to the partner. The goalkeeper then returns to his or her original position and repeats the practice. To vary this practice, different serves should be tried, such as headers and volley kicks.

d. This exercise is essentially the same as exercise c. This time, however, the goalkeeper can also serve and catch in relay games that incorporate heading, volley kicking, and throw-ins.

Technique for Gathering High Balls

When shots or crosses are head high, the goalkeeper gathers the ball as though it were a basketball. The goalkeeper moves directly in front of the ball's flight, arms semiextended and parallel, and palms facing the oncoming ball. Fingers are fully spread, and the thumb and index finger form a W (Figure 11–4). The moment the ball is caught, the goalkeeper withdraws the arms to cushion the shot's power. He or she then repositions the hands and safely gathers the ball into the upper chest.

Practice Exercises

a. A target is placed at about head height on a kickboard. The goalkeeper underhand pitches the ball at the target and catches the rebound. The coach should vary the number of targets and the goalkeeper's position in relation to the board.

b. The goalkeeper practices with a partner. They kneel about three yards from each other. The partner holds the ball in a throw-in position.

Figure 11–4. Practicing for technique gathering an air ball above head height. *Note:* Placement of hands and fingers.

The ball is then thrown to the goalkeeper, who catches it and gathers it into the upper chest. The drill is repeated. Team relays that include heading, volley kicking, and basketball-type games can be incorporated into this exercise.

Technique Vertical Hop

When balls are above head height, such as crosses from the wings, the goalkeeper moves toward the flight of the ball to make the catch. The arms and hands are extended, palms face the oncoming ball, and fingers are spread out to maximize contact. Right before the ball is caught, if there is enough space to maneuver and the ball is high enough, the goalkeeper will execute a vertical hop. He or she pushes off with the strongest jumping foot, catches the ball, and gathers it in at maximum height. (See Figure 11–5.)

Practice Exercises

a. The goalkeeper repeatedly throws a ball high into the air and then takes a one-footed jump to catch and gather the ball.

Figure 11–5. Practicing for technique gathering an air ball. Going up to meet the ball using a one footed vertical hop for maximum height.

b. The goalkeeper throws a ball high against a wall from about five yards away and catches and gathers the rebound. This is repeated.

c. The goalkeeper sits down and holds the ball. He or she then throws the ball high into the air, jumps up, catches and gathers it. This is repeated.

d. The goalkeeper practices with a partner, who stands about ten yards away, holding the ball. The goalkeeper stands about two yards behind a bench that is twelve to eighteen inches high. The partner throws a high ball to the goalie. The goalkeeper makes a one-footed takeoff over the bench, catches and gathers the ball.

e. The goalkeeper may practice with two team players. One team player stands on the goal area line, facing the goalkeeper. The other team player stands six yards behind the goal. The goalkeeper throws the ball. One team player tries to head the ball near, or against, the crossbar. The goalkeeper catches and gathers the ball, then turns and serves it to the other team player. This player volley kicks the ball back toward the crossbar. The goalkeeper catches and gathers the ball, and repeats the procedure. The team players may stand anywhere they wish along the goal area line.

PUNCHING (BOXING) FOR HEIGHT AND DISTANCE

No matter how difficult it is, the goalkeeper must always try to catch and gather the ball. The coach should always discourage attempts to merely knock the ball down or slow its momentum. However, there will be times when it will be impossible to catch the ball. The goalkeeper will have to punch or deflect the ball away from the goal. Punching the ball demands concentration, timing, and courage. In many cases, the goalkeeper must leave the goal to challenge high cross passes among a crowd of players. (Figure 11–6.)

Figure 11–6a. Practicing for technique boxing/punching an air ball when under pressure of an opponent.

Figure 11–6b. Practicing for technique boxing/punching an air ball with both fists when approaching the ball full face on; and under pressure of an opponent. *Note:* Box/punch for height and distance.

Two-Handed Punches

When the flight of the ball draws the goalkeeper forward, the goalkeeper moves directly in front of the ball's flight and uses both fists to punch the ball high in the air and back in the direction whence it came. The fists are placed together to make a wide punching surface, then held in a cocked position across the upper chest and fired up and through the ball. (See Figure 11–6.)

One-Handed Punch

When high crosses drive the goalkeeper backward, he or she must consider fisting the ball with one hand. The goalkeeper moves directly in front of the ball's flight, fist closed and cocked across the upper chest. With a twisting body motion and an overhand swing, the goalkeeper fires the fist up through the ball, propelling it high and wide in the intended direction (Figure 11–7). Most goalkeepers prefer to take off on one foot if there is enough room to run and jump.

Goalkeeping Practice

a. The goalkeeper works with a team player. This player stands about ten yards away, holding a ball. The team player throws the ball toward the goalkeeper, who punches the ball back. This is repeated.

Figure 11–7. Practicing for technique boxing/punching an air ball when driven back across the goal. *Note:* The ball is boxed on in its intended direction with height and distance.

b. The goalkeeper practices with two team players. The second team player has the ball and stands about ten yards away from the first team player. The first team player stands in front of the goalkeeper. The second team player throws the ball high in the air, toward the other team player and the goalkeeper. At the right moment, the goalkeeper makes a one-footed vertical jump and punches the ball clear.

c. The goalkeeper practices with two groups of players, one group of forwards and one group of backs. The forwards stand around the center circle. One player in this group holds a ball. The backs form a smaller inner circle about six yards in diameter. The goalkeeper stands in the middle of the inner circle. The ball is passed as it is in basketball, in any direction, around the outer circle. As soon as the goalkeeper demands the "goalkeeper's ball," the forward in possession of the ball throws it into the inner circle so that the goalkeeper can punch it back out. The backs standing right in front of the passer may attempt to intercept the ball. The players change positions after an allotted amount of time.

d. The goalkeeper practices with two team players. One player holds a ball about ten yards away from the goalkeeper. This player throws the ball high into the air toward the goalkeeper. The goalkeeper sees how far he or she can punch the ball. The other player records the distance with a marker. The goalkeeper must try to beat this distance the next time.

e. Relay teams are formed, each one with its own goalkeeper. The front player throws a ball to the goalkeeper, who is two to ten yards away. The goalkeeper punches the ball so that the last person in line can catch it. The back person moves to the front of the line and play continues until the first player reaches the front position again.

Practice Exercises

a. The goalkeeper works with two team players. One player stands ten yards away on the goalkeeper's right side. The other team player stands the same distance away on the goalkeeper's left side. One player throws a ball in front of the goalkeeper toward the other player. The goalkeeper moves in the direction of the ball's flight, takes a one-footed vertical jump, punches up through the ball, and propels it in the intended direction. Practice is repeated from both sides.

b. Two team players stand in the corners of the goal area box closest to the goal line. One team player throws the ball so that the other team player can head it on goal. The goalkeeper, who stands on the goal line, must one-hand punch the ball over the head of the intended receiver.

DIVING FOR SHOTS

There is nothing more spectacular than seeing a goalkeeper fly through the air to catch or tip away a well-placed shot. But many goalkeepers have problems diving for shots because they're afraid that they will hurt themselves. After all, goalies know that they'll hit the ground after the dive. Thus goals are scored because of the goalkeeper's poor execution. For example, a goalie might hold the ball in one hand and use the other hand to break his or her fall, or dive over the ball to cushion the fall.

There is a proper way to dive for a ground ball that has been forcefully hit to the left or right side of the goalkeeper. The goalkeeper dives sideways in front of the ball's path. The body acts as a barrier, preventing the ball from entering the net. While making the save, the goalkeeper puts one hand behind the ball and the other on top of the ball, securely holding it (Figure 11–8). The goalkeeper gathers the ball into the lower chest and curls up to protect himself or herself from challenging players (Figure 11–8).

Figure 11–8a. Practicing for technique diving for ground balls. Dive and gather in.

Figure 11–8b. If away from goal line roll away from challenging player and tuck up into a neat ball, head tucked in.

Practice Exercises

a. The goalkeeper practices with a team player who stands five yards away and holds the ball. The goalkeeper squats and holds the hands, palms facing out, at the ready position. The team player rolls an underhand ball to one side of the goalkeeper. The moment the ball is released, the goalkeeper falls to the side to make the save.

b. The goalkeeper proceeds as above, except that he or she sits down instead of squatting.

Diving for Ground Balls

When the goalkeeper is diving for ground balls that cannot be held but are within reach, the lower hand must be used to extend the goalie's range. The goalkeeper dives sideways, extends the lower arm and hand, palm out, and pushes the ball away from the goal. (See Figure 11–9.)

Practice Exercises

a. The goalkeeper practices on a kickboard. Two target areas are marked six yards apart at the bottom of the board. The goalkeeper stands between the targets, two yards from the board, holding a ball. He or she rolls the ball toward one of the targets. On the rebound, the goalkeeper dives sideways and deflects the ball. Upon contact with the ball, the lower hand should be locked at a 45-degree angle so that there is no chance of the ball's being pushed back into the field of play toward oncoming attackers.

Figure 11–9. Practicing for technique diving for a ground ball that cannot be held/gathered. *Note:* Lower hand is used for maximum reach.

b. Instead of using a kickboard, the goalkeeper practices with a team player who has a ball at the feet. The goalkeeper squats in front of a bench and faces the team player. The bench's seat forms the ball's target. The team player dribbles the ball toward the goalkeeper and, from three yards out, side foot passes the ball to hit either end of the bench. The moment the ball has been passed, the goalkeeper dives sideways to deflect the ball away from the bench.

Diving for Air Balls

When a well-hit ball is above the ground but below shoulder height, the goalkeeper must try to catch the ball with both hands or push the ball away from the goal. To do this successfully, the goalkeeper must be fearless, acrobatic, and as quick as a cat. As soon as the ball has been kicked, the goalkeeper must react. Only the goalkeeper will know if it is possible to catch the ball. The goalkeeper may have to take a few short steps before diving through the air in order to be positioned behind the ball. To catch the ball, the goalkeeper dives sideways, body fully extended, palms facing the oncoming ball. Once the ball is caught, the entire body curls up in midair. The goalkeeper then lands on the ground, still hugging the ball.

Practice Exercises

a. The goalkeeper works with a team player. The other player holds a ball. The goalkeeper squats, holding the palms of the hands out toward the team player in a W shape. The team player is about three yards away. The team player underhand pitches the ball to the left or right side of the goalkeeper. The goalkeeper dives sideways, catches the ball, and gathers it into the lower chest.

b. The goalkeeper practices with two team players. One team player kneels on all fours, as close to the ground as possible. The goalkeeper stands beside this kneeling player, hands in the ready position, facing the other team player, who is standing. The standing team player holds a ball. This player underhand pitches the ball to the goalkeeper. The goalkeeper makes a diving save by catching (Figure 11–10) or deflecting the ball (Figure 11–11).

c. The goalkeeper practices with three team players. One team player stands at the intersection of the goal line and the penalty-area line, with a ball at the feet. The second team player stands in front of the middle of the goal, near the penalty spot. The third team player kneels down parallel to the goal line on all fours, close to the ground and just outside the near goal post. The goalkeeper covers the near post. The player with the ball dribbles along the goal line toward the intersection of the goal area line

Figure 11–10. Practicing for technique diving for an air ball using a partner to assist in proper diving technique.

and the goal line, and kicks the ball in front of the goal. The second team player has moved toward the goal and is waiting for the centering cross. The goalkeeper dives sideways toward the goal and over the kneeling player. The goalie either catches and gathers the ball or pushes the ball away from the awaiting player. Note: Instead of kicking the ball, the first team player might underhand pitch the ball in front of the goal to the awaiting player. This player will be standing on the goal area line, in front of the middle of the goal. The goalkeeper dives sideways toward the goal and over the kneeling player, either to catch the ball or deflect it.

Lower Hand for Maximum Distance

Sometimes balls are above the ground but below shoulder height. They cannot be caught but are within the goalkeeper's reach. The lower hand must be used to control these balls. (See Figure 11–11.)

Practice Exercises

a. The goalkeeper works with a team player. The goalkeeper stands on the goal line, central to the goal. A tether ball is hung from the cross bar, two feet above the ground and one foot from the goalpost. The team player takes the ball and moves infield until the tether ball line is taut. When the goalkeeper is ready, the team player releases the ball. The goalkeeper dives sideways and deflects the ball away from the goal.

To vary this practice, the goalkeeper practices with a team player

Figure 11–11. Practicing for technique diving for an air ball that cannot be gathered in. *Note:* Lower hand is used for maximum reach and deflection.

Figure 11–12. Practicing for technique diving for an air ball above head height that cannot be gathered in. *Note:* Upper hand is used for maximum height and deflection.

who holds a ball. The goalkeeper stands on the goal line central to the goal, facing infield. The team player stands one yard from the goal line, one foot from the upright, and faces the goal. The team player releases the ball from chest height. The goalkeeper deflects the ball. (Figure 11–12.)

Figure 11–13. Practicing for technique diving at an opponent's feet. *Note:* Head down behind arms for protection.

Diving for Balls Above Head Height

When one is diving for balls that are above head height, the upper hand should be used for maximum reach. (See Figure 11–13.)

Practice Exercises

a. The goalkeeper practices with two team players. One team player holds a ball and faces the goalkeeper. This player is four yards away from the goalie, at approximately a 45-degree angle to the near goal post. The goalkeeper is within arm's length of the near post and faces the first team player. The second team player stands two yards infield, across from the far post. The team player with the ball full instep volley kicks it just above the goalkeeper's head and in front of the goal, toward the second team player. The goalkeeper side steps toward the ball, pushes up off the lead foot, and twists the body in the air to follow the ball's path. The upper arm is semiextended, the palm underneath the ball. The arm is thrust through the ball, pushing it toward the second team player.

b. The practice proceeds as above, only this time the team player with the ball underhand pitches it instead of volley kicking it.

c. The goalkeeper practices with two team players. Two benches are placed on top of each other, and wrestling mats are placed on either side of the benches. The goalkeeper stands beside the benches, which are two yards away. One team player holds a ball and stands about four yards away, at a 45-degree angle to the goalkeeper. The second team player stands diagonally across from and four yards behind the goalkeeper. The first team player underhand pitches the ball above head height, past the goalkeeper and toward the second team player. The goalkeeper pushes off with the lead foot up and over the benches, twists his or her body, and deflects the ball high and wide with the palm of the hand.

Technique Diving at an Opponent's Feet

Diving at an opponent's feet demands courage and timing. Without this tactic, however, it would be a waste of time to teach goalkeeping techniques. The goalkeeper must be naturally aggressive and daring to become a respected member of the team. (Figure 11–13.)

Practice Exercises

a. The goalkeeper practices with a team player who has a ball at the feet. The team player stands one yard away from the goalkeeper and faces him or her. The goalkeeper crouches, body weight forward, palms facing out, and eyes fixed on the ball. The team player raises his or her leg as if he or she is going to kick the ball. The moment the leg is raised, the goalkeeper dives sideways across the team player to smother the ball. Whenever possible, the goalkeeper rolls over with his or her back to the team player. This prevents any serious injury that might result from an errant kick. (See Figure 11–13.)

b. The goalkeeper practices with four team players, each of whom has a ball at the feet. The team players stand on the goal area line about three yards apart, with their backs to the goal. The goalkeeper stands in a ready position two yards behind the first team player on the left side. The goalkeeper calls for the player to shoot. The moment the team player starts to pivot, the goalkeeper dives sideways toward the player and blocks the shot.

c. The goalkeeper practices with a team player. Four soccer balls are placed on the goal area line, one yard apart. The goalkeeper and the team player stand facing each other over the first ball, approximately two yards apart. On a given signal, the team player attempts to shoot the balls one by one into the goal. The goalkeeper tries to block as many of the shots as possible. He or she dives sideways to smother the first two balls. Then the goalkeeper partially rises and dives once again to try to smother the remaining two balls.

d. The goalkeeper practices with a team player. The team player stands at the top of the penalty-area, with a ball at the feet. The goalkeeper stands in the goal, facing the team player. The team player dribbles the ball toward the goal. The goalkeeper advances from the goal line to challenge the oncoming player. The team player tries to dribble past the goalkeeper and place the ball on the goal line. The goalkeeper closes in, shepherds the team player away from the goal, and dives to smother the ball.

ANTICIPATING AND CONTROLLING

Understanding Angles

Understanding angles makes for sound goalkeeping. The experienced goalkeeper rarely loses positional awareness when called upon to leave the goal line and challenge for the ball. The goalkeeper knows precisely where he or she is in relationship to the goalpost and to other players. The goalie often uses markings within the penalty-area to retain a sense of position. The goalkeeper who always stands on the goal line sacrifices his or her greatest advantage—the right to use the hands within the penalty-area. Through practice and match play, the goalkeeper will develop the ability to anticipate and cut off dangerous passes on the edge of the penalty-area, and even outside it.

Many goalkeepers patrol the front of the penalty-area, moving and changing position as the direction of play changes. If the play approaches the attacking third of the field, the goalkeeper retreats within the goal area to avoid being caught by a surprise high shot.

When an opponent is in a shooting position, the goalkeeper's main concern is to present the smallest possible target. The goalkeeper who stands on the goal line in front of the middle of the goalpost presents the largest possible target (Figure 11–14). As the goalkeeper moves forward to challenge an opponent, the visible target area is reduced (Figure 11–15). If the opponent advances toward the goal from an angle, the area of the target is reduced even further as the goalkeeper advances.

Mistakes that most often occur are as follows:

1. The goalkeeper makes no effort to close down the greatest possible area.
2. The goalkeeper advances too soon and too far, leaving the ball carrier with the options of passing the ball to another player, or chipping the ball over the goalkeeper's head into the goal.
3. The goalkeeper recklessly charges the ball carrier, making it easy for the ball carrier to dribble the ball around him or her.

Practice Exercises

a. The goalkeeper practices with a team player. The player stands on the penalty spot holding a rope that is tied to each goalpost. The rope

Figure 11–14. Practicing for technique understanding angles. *Note:* Too much of the goal presented to the attacker.

Figure 11–15. Utilizing rope to improve goalkeeper's understanding of angles. *Note:* Goalkeeper's position now has restricted target area.

thus forms a triangle. The goalkeeper moves toward the team player, arms extended, palms facing infield. The goalkeeper stops only when his or her hands are directly over the rope. At this point, the possibilities of a shot into the goal will have been reduced to a minimum. (See Figure 11–20.) Note: The team player may move across the face of the goal with the rope, presenting the goalkeeper with different angles. The goalkeeper then advances to further reduce the target area.

b. The goalkeeper practices with six to eight team players. The ends of a rope are tied to the goalposts, and the center is pegged into the ground at the top corner of the penalty-area, to form a triangle. The goalkeeper stands on the goal line, facing the team players. The first team player advances inside the triangle toward the goal and attempts to shoot into the goal. The goalkeeper advances cautiously through the triangle to reduce the target area to its smallest size. To vary this practice, the rope is moved across the front of the penalty-area to present the goalkeeper with different angles. The team players attempt to dribble the ball around the goalkeeper.

Clearing the Ball

When in possession of the ball, the goalkeeper continually kicks it as high and as far downfield as possible. This can cause less skilled players many problems when they are trying to control the ball. The time will come when this tactic will work against the goalkeeper. If the opposition continuously regains possession of the ball and counterattacks, the goalkeeper will be very busy. Once in possession of the ball, the goalkeeper should start an attack with an accurate kick, pass, or throw that can be readily controlled by a team player.

Practice Exercises

a. The goalkeeper practices against a kickboard. The ball is placed six yards away from the board. The goalkeeper steps three to four yards back, at a slight angle to the ball. The goalkeeper then approaches the ball. The last stride he or she takes before making contact with the ball should be long. This will ensure a maximum leg swing and good height and distance (Figure 11–16). The nonkicking foot is slightly behind the ball. The kicking foot strikes through the ball along the inner side of the shoelaces. This is the instep kick. The ball is lifted high up on the rebound surface.

b. The goalkeeper practices with a team player. The goalkeeper places the ball at the front corner of the goal area box and then stands by the goalpost that is closest to the ball. The team player stands near the touchline, ten yards away from the front of the penalty-area. The goalkeeper tries to kick the ball to the team player.

c. The goalkeeper practices with six to eight team players. The team players form a large arc across the center of the field, facing the goalkeeper. The goalkeeper holds a ball and calls a team player by name. From the front of the penalty-area, the goalkeeper volley kicks the ball to this team player. (See Figure 11–17.)

Figure 11–16. Practicing for technique the goal kick.
Note: High leg lift and follow through.

Figure 11–17. Practicing for technique punting the ball.
Note: Body weight back from the ball, drive through the ball with good follow through.

    d. The goalkeeper practices with two team players. The players place four markers on either side of the penalty-area. The markers form two ten-yard-by-ten-yard squares. These squares are located about ten yards downfield from the front of the penalty-area, near the touchline. From within the penalty-area, the goalkeeper attempts to volley kick the ball on

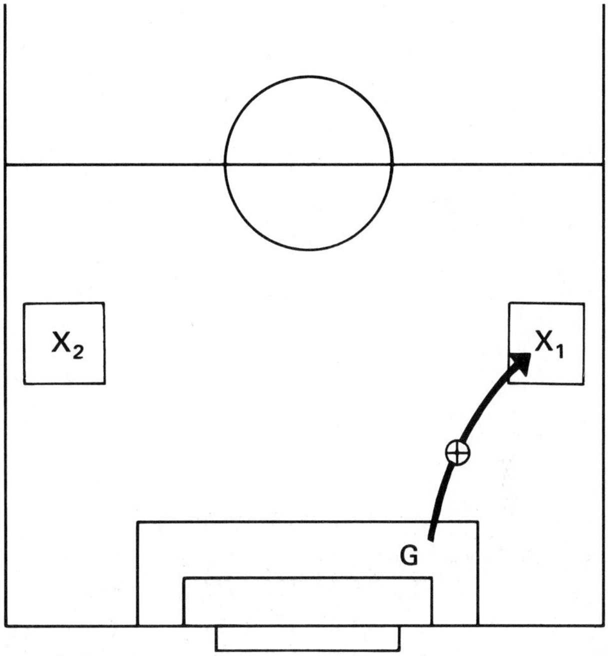

Figure 11–18. Functional training to improve technique, punting for direction and distance.

Figure 11–19. Practicing for technique distributing the ball underhand.

the first bounce into either of the squares. The ball is then controlled by the team players, who dribble it and shoot at the goalkeeper. The players then return to their respective grids. (See Figure 11–19.)

e. The goalkeeper practices with a team player. This player stands at the top corner of the penalty-area, with a ball at the feet. The goalkeeper

Figure 11–20. Practicing for technique distributing the ball overhand. *Note:* The goalkeeper propels the ball down towards supporting player's feet.

stands in the goal area, facing the team player. The team player dribbles the ball toward the goalkeeper. When the player is four to five yards away from the goalie, he or she passes the ball so that the goalkeeper can gather it. The player then sprints back to the original spot, turns, and calls for the ball. The goalkeeper, with a bowling action, rolls the ball to the team player. (See Figure 11–18.)

f. The goalkeeper practices with two team players. One team player stands in front of the penalty-area, with a ball at the feet. The second team player stands near the halfway line, close to the touchline. The goalkeeper stands in the goal area, facing the team player with the ball. The player with the ball dribbles and shoots at the goalkeeper. The second team player also moves down the touchline toward the goalkeeper. The goalkeeper promptly pitches the ball overhand to the second team player, who faces the goal. (See Figure 11–20.)

Most of the practice exercises presented in this chapter can be easily modified to suit all ages and types of players. Using a kickboard or wall during practice sessions will greatly aid the young, novice goalkeeper's development. Remember, however, that there is no experience like game play. The goalkeeper must be included in all individual, group, and team activities.

CHAPTER TWELVE

Conditioned Games to Improve Technique

Conditioned games that improve playing technique are invaluable, especially when mental and physical fatigue is affecting the team's or individual players' performance. When players fail to apply basic techniques, move sluggishly, or daydream often, it is time to change the demands and pressures of the training program. The coach must offer the players something different and less demanding, yet closely related to the game of soccer. Conditioned games are designed to help the coach cope on days when the players fail to respond to the designated program. These games are also fun warm-ups, requiring little or no equipment. They can be adapted for use with players of all ages.

In these games, the coach is strictly a low key figure. The coach acts as an umpire, advisor, and demonstrator of the conditions imposed on the players in the games. The coach might want to participate in some of the games. After all, coaches sometimes need a little rejuvenation too. The coach should try to refrain from demanding quality work; rather, he or she should encourage the team by praising any noteworthy efforts of players.

The games should be introduced into the training program on a rotating basis during the course of the season. They can be continued and modified until the coach is satisfied that the team's mental and physical awareness has improved.

KNOCK-OUT SOCCER TENNIS

Knock-out soccer tennis is a game for players of all ages. The game can be adapted to suit the needs of the novice player or the more advanced player.

The game demands little in the way of equipment and field space. The number of players participating can be as few as eight or as many as twenty-four, depending on the number of courts available. The coach must be in a position to observe the players and gain their attention at all times.

KNOCK-OUT SOCCER TENNIS *Situation 1*

Age Group   Ten to twelve years.

Number of Players   Even number per court (not less than six or more than ten).

Time   Ten minutes per court (total game time not to exceed thirty minutes).

Layout of Playing Area   See Figure 12–1.

Equipment   For each tennis court, one soccer ball (size four if available), one pair net supports. If courts are not available, team benches, hurdles, cones or sim-

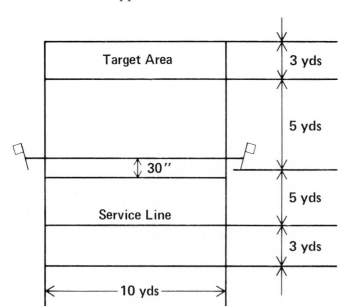

Figure 12–1. Layout for soccer tennis.

ilar markers can be used to mark off the court area. If courts are not available, the coach marks off the required number of courts using available equipment. (See Figure 12–1.) The players are then divided into groups A and B and assigned to courts.

Method of Play

The same number of players stands at either end of the court. (See Figure 12–2.) The player with the soccer ball, A_1, stands on the service line and releases the ball. Without letting it bounce, A_1 instep volley kicks the ball over the net, into the target area. The moment the ball has been kicked by player A_1, receiver B_1, standing on the baseline, moves into the target area to catch the ball before it bounces. If server A_1 fails to volley kick the soccer ball into the target area, he or she is knocked out of the game. If receiver B_1 fails to catch the soccer ball, he or she is knocked out of the game. If kicker A_1 and receiver B_1 are successful in their tasks, each joins the group of players at the opposite end of the court. The game continues until someone wins.

Rules

1. Server A_1 is allowed two service attempts.
2. Net serves must be retaken.
3. The ball can be kicked into any part of the target area.
4. A coin toss decides who will serve.

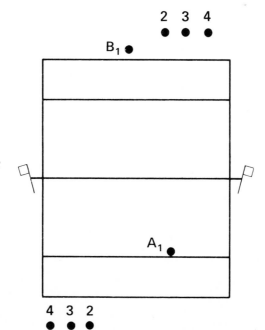

Figure 12–2. Layout for soccer tennis.

Conditions Imposed on Players	Only full instep volley kicking is allowed.
Effect of Game	It improves the full instep volley kick technique and the goalkeeper gathering technique. It also improves each player's feel for the ball's distance and direction.
Suggestion	Player A_1 takes a throw-in into the target area. Receiver B_1 lies on his or her stomach facing A_1. The moment player A_1 releases the ball, B_1 jumps up to catch it in the target area before it bounces. (Same rules apply.)

KNOCK-OUT SOCCER TENNIS *Situation 2*

Age Group	Thirteen to fifteen years.
Number of Players	Same as in situation 1.
Time	Same as in situation 1.
Layout of Playing Area	See Figure 12–1.
Equipment	Same as in situation 1, except use a size five ball.
Method of Play	The same number of players stands at either end of the court. (See Figure 12–2.) Player A_1, standing on the service line, releases the ball, lets it bounce, and full volley kicks it over the net, into the target area. As soon as the ball is kicked, receiver B_1, standing on the baseline, moves into the target area and sole foot traps the ball before it bounces.
Rules	1. Player A_1 is allowed two service attempts.
	2. Net serves must be retaken.
	3. If player A_1 fails to volley kick the soccer ball into the target area, he or she is knocked out of the game.
	4. If receiver B_1 fails to sole foot trap the ball, he or she is knocked out of the game.
	5. If both players A_1 and receiver B_1 are successful, they join the groups of players on the other side of the court.
	6. The game continues until there is a winner.
	7. The ball can be volley kicked into any part of the target area.
	8. After completion of the sole foot trap, the ball is given to a newly designated server.

Conditions Imposed on Players	Full instep kicking only, sole foot trap only.
Effect of Game	It improves the players' sole foot trapping technique and encourages players to move onto the ball. It also improves the full instep kicking technique for weight and accuracy.
Suggestions	a. Receivers thigh trap. b. Receivers chest trap.

KNOCK-OUT SOCCER TENNIS *Situation 3*

Age Group	Sixteen to eighteen
Number of Players	Same as in situation 1.
Time	Same as in situation 1
Layout of Playing Area	See Figure 12–3.
Equipment	Same as in situation 2.

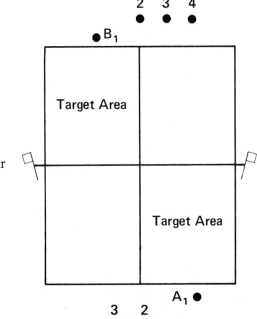

Figure 12–3. Layout for soccer tennis.

Method of Play

The same number of players stands at either end of the court. (See Figure 12–3.) Player A_1 standing on the baseline, releases the ball, and when it bounces, volley kicks it over the net, into the service area. Player A_1 then runs to the other side of the court and joins group B. Receiver B_1 moves from the baseline into the court. B_1 can either head the ball over the net and into the far court, or let it bounce once and then instep ball juggle toward the net, before heading the ball over the net. B_1 then joins group A. This continues until only two players remain. Then, receiver B_1 plays the ball back over the net with enough height so that he or she can run to the other side and again play the ball over the net to A. A will have raced to the spot vacated by B. This continues until someone is knocked out.

Rules

1. The server is allowed only one service attempt.

2. Net serves must be retaken.

3. Only the service must be played into the target areas.

4. Players A or B are knocked out of the game if: (a) they fail to serve the ball into the target area; (b) they fail to keep the ball within the boundaries of the court; or (c) they allow the ball to bounce more than once.

5. Service attempts may be taken from either end of the court.

6. An even number of players must be on both sides of the court at all times.

7. A coin toss will decide which of the last two remaining players will serve the ball.

Conditions Imposed on Players

Only heading and instep juggling are allowed.

Effect of Game

It improves the players' instep kicking, heading, and feel for the ball.

Suggestions

After the ball bounces once, receivers can ball juggle with the head, thigh, or any other part of the body, and then side foot volley the ball over the net.

SOCCER CRICKET

Soccer cricket is similar to soccer baseball. The game can be played by players of all ages and skill levels. The skills required of players may range from basic instep kicking to a more advanced combination of controlling and passing techniques.

The game demands little in the way of equipment and field space. Anywhere from six to eighteen players may participate at once.

SOCCER CRICKET *Situation 1*

Age Group   Ten to twelve years.

Number of   Six to twelve.
Players

Time   Twenty to thirty minutes.

Layout of   See Figure 12–4.
Playing Area

Equipment   One size four soccer ball; two cones or sweat tops.

Method of   The coach places one marker, M_1, on the touchline, and another marker,
Play M_2, twelve paces away from M_1. The team goalkeeper stands at marker
                   M_2 and holds a ball. The other players are given batting order numbers
                   and are positioned as shown in Figure 12–5. The game begins when the
                   goalkeeper underhand rolls the ball toward batter B_1. B_1 stands in front of
                   marker M_1. B_1 instep kicks the ball as hard as possible in any direction

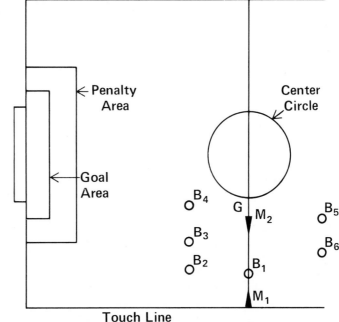

Figure 12–4. Layout for soccer cricket situation 1.

O = Players in Batting Order
▲ = Markers Placed Approximately 10 yds Apart
G = Goalkeeper

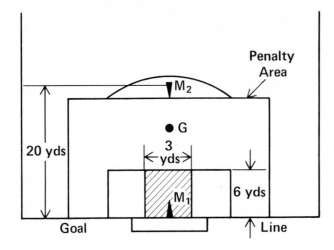

Figure 12–5. Layout for soccer cricket situation 2.

 = Target Box

⬥ = Markers

● = Penalty Spot

infield from the touchline. As soon as the ball has been kicked, batter B_1 runs to touch marker M_2. At the same time, the fielder closest to the ball gathers it up and full instep volley kicks it back to the goalkeeper, who tries to tag the batter with the ball.

Rules

1. Each batter receives six pitches.

2. The batter must run once the ball has been kicked.

3. A goal is scored if the batter touches marker M_2 before being tagged with the ball by the goalkeeper.

4. If the batter is tagged before reaching marker M_2 the batter is "out," and is replaced by the next batter.

5. If the fielders have difficulty retrieving the ball, the batter can keep running and gain another goal every time one of the markers is touched.

6. If the batter successfully touches marker M_2 for a score, the batter is allowed to walk back to marker M_2.

7. The winner is the player who accumulates the highest number of goals in six deliveries.

Conditions Imposed on Players

1. Batters must attempt to instep kick the ball on the ground.

2. Fielders must full volley kick the ball out of their hands.

3. Goalkeepers must roll the ball underhand.

Effect of Game	It improves the instep and full volley kicks. It also develops the goalkeeper's gathering and distribution technique. The players' speed off the mark and mental alertness are developed.
Suggestions	Fielders control the ball with the sole, outside, and inside of the foot.

SOCCER CRICKET *Situation 2*

Age Group	Thirteen to fifteen years.
Number of Players	Six to twelve players.
Time	Thirty minutes.
Layout of Playing Area	Increase the distance between the markers M_1 and M_2 to twenty paces. (See Figures 12–5 and 12–6.)
Method of Play	The coach places marker M_1 on the goal line. Marker M_2 is placed twenty paces infield, beyond the front of the penalty-area. The goalkeeper stands on the penalty spot and holds a ball. The other team players are given batting order numbers. Play commences when the goalkeeper underhand

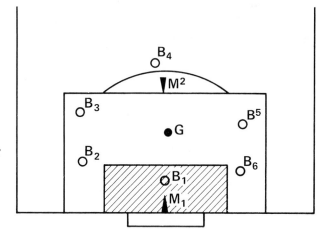

Figure 12–6. Layout for soccer cricket situation 2.

bounces the ball into the goal area target box, in front of batter B_1. As soon as the ball is released, batter B_1 moves toward the ball, sole foot traps it, and instep kicks it in front of the goal area line. Batter B_1 runs to touch marker M_2. At the same time, the fielder closest to the ball controls it with the side of the foot. The fielder dribbles the ball back to the goalkeeper, who covers marker M_2.

Rules

1. Each batter receives six pitches only.
2. The batter must run once the ball has been kicked.
3. The ball must be instep kicked along the ground.
4. The goalkeeper must pitch the ball underhand into the target box.
5. The batter is declared "out" if tagged before touching markers M_1 or M_2.
6. A goal is scored every time the batter touches the markers.
7. Any number of goals may be scored while the fielders are retrieving and dribbling the ball back to the goalkeeper.
8. The goalkeeper must tag the batter while holding the ball.
9. The winner is the batter who accumulates the highest number of goals.

Conditions Imposed on Players

1. Batters must try to sole foot trap the ball.
2. Batters must instep kick the ball along the ground.
3. Fielders must control the ball with the side of the foot.
4. Fielders must dribble the ball at speed and with good control.
5. The goalkeeper must underhand pitch the ball.

Effect of Game

Improves the players' instep kicking, dribbling, and control. It also improves the goalkeeper's distribution technique.

Suggestion

Batter B may full instep volley kick the ball once it has bounced in the target box. The fielders must try to control the ball with the sole of the foot. If they are successful in the execution of the sole foot trap, batter B is declared "out." Otherwise, all the same rules apply.

SOCCER CRICKET *Situation 3*

Age Group

Sixteen to eighteen years.

Number of Players

Two teams (forwards and backs).

Time	Thirty minutes.
Layout of Playing Area	See Figure 12–7.
Equipment	Same as situation 1, except size five ball is used.
Method of Play	The coach places marker M_1 at the top of the center circle in one half of the field, and marker M_2 at the top of the circle in the other half of the field. The goalkeeper stands at marker M_2, holding a ball. A coin toss determines which team bats first. Batting order numbers are assigned. Batter B_1 stands in front of marker M_1. The rest of the batting team members retire to another part of the field to practice until they are called upon to bat. The fielders position themselves in a circle around markers M_1 and M_2. The goalkeeper overhand pitches the ball toward batter B_1. B_1 must head the ball high in any direction, then run to touch marker M_2. The fielder closest to the ball plays the ball the first time (one touch), or relay passes it back, through the other fielders, to the goalkeeper at marker M_2.

Rules

1. Each batter receives six good pitches.

2. The goalkeeper must pitch the ball above shoulder height and within the circle.

3. Batter B must run once the ball has been headed.

4. A run is scored if batter B touches markers M_2 and M_1 before the ball is returned to the goalkeeper.

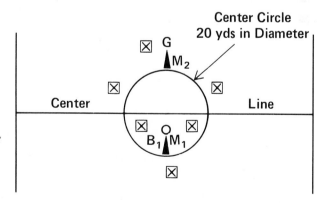

Figure 12–7. Layout for soccer cricket situation 3.

O = Batting Team
X = Fielding Team
▲ = Markers
G = Goalkeeper

5. Batter B is out if he is tagged by the goalkeeper before reaching marker M_1 or M_2.

6. Back headers are in.

7. The team accumulating the highest number of runs is the winner.

Conditions Imposed on Players

1. The batters must attempt to head for height and distance.

2. The fielders must first time pass the ball.

3. The goalkeeper must pitch the ball underhand.

Effect of Game

It improves the players' heading and passing skills, as well as the goalkeeper's gathering and distribution technique.

Suggestions

a. Whenever possible, fielders may catch the head ball to make an out.

b. The fielders must control the ball using the chest, thigh, or foot before instep passing back to the goalkeeper.

SOCCER BASEBALL

SOCCER BASEBALL *Situation 1*

Age Group

Ten to twelve years.

Number of Players

Two teams (forwards and backs).

Time

Thirty minutes.

Layout of Playing Area

See Figure 12–8.

Equipment

One size four soccer ball; three cones or sweat tops.

Method of Play

The coach places markers M_1, M_2, and M_3 around the penalty-area, and divides the players into two teams of forwards and backs. A coin toss determines which team will bat first. The team goalkeeper stands at marker M_2 and holds a ball. Fielders are placed in regular baseball positions. Batter B_1 stands beside the penalty spot (home plate), inside the target box. The goalkeeper underhand pitches the ball along the ground to batter B_1. B_1 instep kicks the ball into the playing area and runs to the appropriate base. The fielder closest to the ball controls it with the sole, inside, or outside of the foot. The fielder then gathers up the ball and full instep volley kicks it out of the hands to the appropriate base fielder.

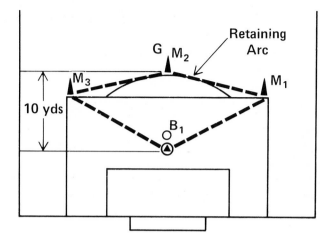

Figure 12–8. Layout for soccer baseball situation 1.

▲ = Markers
◉ = Home Base (Penalty Spot)
O = Batting Team
G = Goalkeeper

Rules

1. Batter B receives only one pitch.
2. The goalkeeper must pitch the ball underhand along the ground, and within the target box. If the ball misses the target box, batter B receives another pitch.
3. The fielder must control the ball with the foot before gathering it up to volley kick.
4. A run is scored every time a batter crosses home plate safely.
5. The batter must be tagged with the ball for an out.
6. Every three outs, the teams change positions.
7. No team may bat for more than five minutes at a time.
8. The team that gains the highest number of runs in the allotted time wins.

Conditions Imposed on Players

1. The goalkeeper must underhand pitch the ball.
2. The fielders must try to control the ball with the sole, inside, or outside of the foot.
3. The fielders must try to instep volley kick the ball out of their hands.
4. Batters must try to full instep kick the ball.

Effect of Game	It improves players' ball control and instep and volley kicking techniques. It also improves the goalkeeper's distribution.
Suggestions	a. When the goalkeeper rolls the ball into the target box, batter B instep kicks the ball with the weaker foot.
	b. After the ball has been controlled by the fielder, the same fielder dribbles it to the appropriate base.

SOCCER BASEBALL *Situation 2*

Age Group	Thirteen to fifteen years.
Number of Players	Two teams (forwards and backs).
Time	Thirty minutes.
Layout of Playing Area	See Figure 12–9.
Equipment	One size five soccer ball, three cones or sweat tops for markers.
Method of Play	The coach places markers M_1, M_2, M_3, and M_4 around the penalty-area, and divides the players into two teams of forwards and backs. A coin toss determines which team bats first. The goalkeeper stands twelve yards

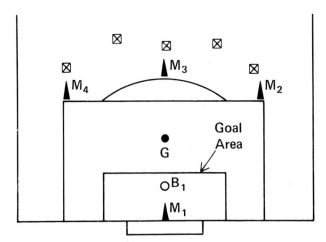

Figure 12–9. Layout for soccer baseball situation 2.

▲ = Markers
⊠ = Fielding Team
○ = Batting Team
G = Goalkeeper

away at the penalty spot and holds a ball. Fielders are placed in regular baseball positions. Batter B$_1$ stands in front of the middle of the goal on the goal line. The goalkeeper underhand pitches the ball high enough for the batter to execute a thigh trap. Once the batter has thigh trapped the ball, he or she may full instep volley kick it before it bounces or let it bounce once and then full instep volley kick it. The batter then runs to the appropriate base. The fielder closest to the ball controls it with the sole of the foot on the first or second bounce, and then instep or side foot passes the ball.

Rules

1. The batter receives only one pitch unless, in the coach's opinion, the ball's delivery made it impossible for the batter to execute a proper thigh trap.
2. The batter must run once the ball has been volley kicked.
3. The batter or the marker may be tagged for an out.
4. A run is scored every time a batter crosses home plate safely.
5. No team may bat for more than five minutes at a time.
6. The team with the highest number of runs wins the game.

Conditions Imposed on Players

1. The batter must try to thigh trap the ball.
2. Fielders must try to sole foot trap the ball.
3. Fielders must try to instep or side foot pass the ball.
4. The goalkeeper must underhand pitch the ball.

Effect of Game

It improves air ball control, instep and side foot passing technique, and volley kicking technique.

Suggestions

a. The goalkeeper must catch the volley kick before it bounces to make an out.
b. Field players control the ball by running through the ball.
c. A field player serves the ball as a regular throw-in.

SOCCER BASEBALL *Situation 3*

Age Group   Sixteen to eighteen years.

Number of Players   Two teams (forwards and backs).

Time   Thirty minutes.

Layout of Playing Area   See Figure 12–10.

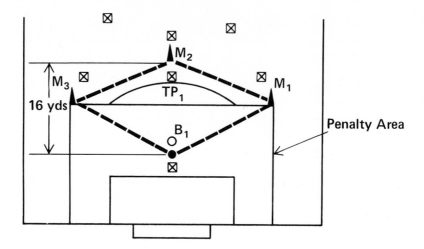

▲ = Markers
⊠ = Fielding Team
○ = Batting Team
● = Home Base (Penalty Spot)

Figure 12–10. Layout for soccer baseball situation 3.

Equipment
One size five soccer ball, three cones or sweat tops for markers.

Method of Play
The coach places markers M_1, M_2, and M_3 in position around the penalty-area. Two teams of forwards and backs are selected. A coin toss determines which team will bat first. A team player stands at the top of the penalty-area, facing the penalty spot. Batter B_1 stands behind the penalty spot. The goalkeeper is the catcher. Team player TP_1 serves a regular throw-in that batter B_1 must chest trap and then sole foot trap as the ball hits the ground. Batter B_1 then instep passes the ball into the field of play and runs to first base. The fielder closest to the ball controls it with the sole, inside, or outside of the foot. The fielder then instep or side foot passes the ball back to the appropriate base.

Rules
1. The batter receives only one delivery, unless, in the coach's opinion, the ball's delivery made it impossible for the batter to execute a proper chest trap.
2. The batter must run once the ball has been instep kicked.
3. The batter or the marker may be tagged for an out.
4. A run is scored every time a batter safely crosses home plate.
5. No team may bat for more than five minutes at a time.

6. The team that gains the highest number of runs in the allotted time wins.

Conditions Imposed on Players

1. The batter must try to chest and sole foot trap the ball.
2. All players side foot or instep pass the ball.
3. Server TP must make a proper throw-in.

Effect of Game

It improves players' control of air balls as well as their passing technique.

Suggestions

a. The batter heads the ball into the field of play.
b. The fielder dribbles the ball back to the appropriate marker with the weak foot.
c. The fielders sit down, and the batter executes a diving header. The fielder closest to the ball jumps up, controls the ball with any part of the body, and then passes the ball to the appropriate base.

SOCCER BALL KNOCK-OUT

SOCCER BALL KNOCK-OUT *Situation 1*

Age Group

Ten to twelve years.

Number of Players

Twelve to eighteen players (even number per circle).

Time

Twelve to fifteen minutes (two minutes per pair).

Layout of Playing Area

See Figure 12–11 (two circles).

Equipment

Two size four soccer balls.

Method of Play

All players stand in the center circle. Two players, O_1 and O_2, have balls at their feet. Play commences when players O_1 and O_2 begin to dribble their balls with the inside and outside of their feet around the inside of the center circle. The other players also move around the inside of the circle, hopping on one foot, dodging, and weaving. They want to avoid being tagged by ball carriers O_1 and O_2. Each pair of ball carriers has one minute to try to tag as many players as possible.

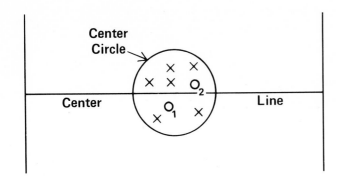

Figure 12–11. Layout for soccer ball knock-out situation 1.

X = Team Players
O = Players Dribbling the Ball

Rules	1. Any player who does not stay inside of the circle is knocked out of the game.
	2. The ball carrier must be in possession of the ball when tagging team players.
	3. All players must be given the chance to dribble the ball.
Conditions Imposed on Players	1. Ball carriers must try to dribble the ball with both the inside and outside of the foot.
	2. Players must be moving at all times.
Effect of Game	It improves the players' dribbling technique and tactical awareness. It also improves the players' speed off the mark and lateral movement.
Suggestions	a. Divide players into forwards and backs. The forward player with the ball must try to tag back players, and the back player with the ball must try to tag forwards. The ball carrier who tags more members of the opposing team in the shortest amount of time, or in one minute, wins.
	b. If they are tagged, fielders must sit down. However, they can resume play if they can successfully use their hands to push the ball away from the ball carrier's feet when the ball carrier's attention wanders.

SOCCER BALL KNOCK-OUT *Situation 2*

Age Group	Thirteen to fifteen years.
Number of Players	Twelve to eighteen (two teams, forwards and backs).

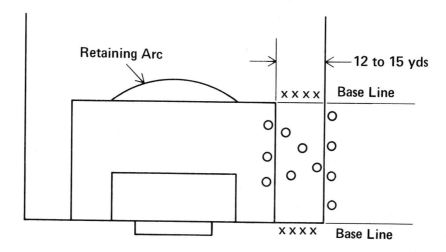

x = **Team Players with a Ball**
O = **Team Players Challenging** x

Figure 12–12. Layout for soccer ball knock-out situation 2.

Time	Fifteen minutes.
Layout of Playing Area	See Figure 12–12.
Equipment	Eight or ten size five soccer balls, and four cones or sweat tops for markers.
Method of Play	The coach marks off an area adjacent to the penalty-area, and divides the players into forwards and backs. A coin toss determines which team has the balls and which team will challenge for the balls. The team in possession of the balls splits into two groups. The groups stand on the baseline, at the top and bottom of the grid, with the balls at their feet. The challengers also divide into two groups. One group stands in the middle of the grid. The remaining challengers stand on both sides of the grid. Both groups of offensive players dribble their balls through the grid, trying to reach the other side of the grid safely. Challengers in the middle of the grid try to kick the ball out from under the feet of the ball carriers. Challengers on the sidelines may reach into the playing area, but only to kick the ball away. An offensive player is knocked out of the game if his or her ball is kicked out of the grid. After all the ball carriers have been knocked out, the teams change positions.
Rules	1. The ball carriers must stay within the boundaries of the grid.

2. The ball carriers must cross the grid from baseline to baseline.

3. The ball carrier who crosses from base to base the greatest number of times is declared the winner.

Conditions Imposed on Players

1. The ball carriers must try to use the inside and outside of the foot when dribbling and screening.

2. The challengers must only use the front and side block tackles.

Effect of Game

It improves the players' dribbling and closing down techniques, tactical awareness, and tackling ability.

Suggestions

a. The challenger in the middle of the grid becomes the new ball carrier if he or she gains the ball as the result of a good tackle or because of the ball carrier's poor control. The player who loses the ball is replaced by one of the challengers standing along the sidelines. These challengers have been assigned numbers.

b. All players stand in the grid in pairs. One member of each pair has a ball at the feet, and the other player is his or her shadow. The ball carriers all have numbers. The ball carriers dribble inside the grid in any direction, followed by their shadows. The coach calls out one of the given numbers. The ball carrier assigned that particular number must dribble the ball over one of the baselines, while his or her partner tries to win the ball.

SOCCER BALL KNOCK-OUT *Situation 3*

Age Group

Sixteen to eighteen years.

Number of Players

Twelve to eighteen (or groups according to the number of balls available).

Time

Fifteen minutes.

Layout of Playing Area

See Figure 12–13.

Equipment

One size five soccer ball per player.

Method of Play

The players stand in the center circle with balls at their feet. The coach assigns the following numbers to these dribbling techniques: one is pushing the ball with the sole of the foot; two is dragging the ball sideways with the sole of the foot; three is dribbling the ball with the inside and outside of the foot; and four is dragging the ball backwards with the sole of the foot. All the players randomly dribble the balls. When the coach

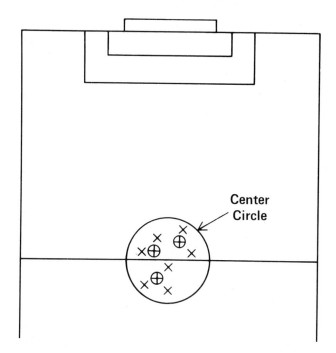

Center
Circle

Figure 12–13. Layout for soccer ball knock-out situation 3.

× = Team Players
⊕ = Ball

calls out one of the assigned numbers, the players react by executing the specified task. Players who do not respond correctly are knocked out of the game. The last player to remain is the winner.

Rules

1. Players responding with the incorrect technique are knocked out of the game.
2. Players colliding with each other are knocked out of the game.
3. Players drifting outside of the circle are knocked out of the game.

Conditions Imposed on Players

The players must try to use all the dribbling techniques.

Effect of Game

It improves players' dribbling techniques and makes them more alert.

Suggestions

a. The players dribble the ball in the circle. On a given signal, they try to kick the other players' balls out of the circle while screening their own ball. The winner is the player who is still dribbling and screening when every other player has been knocked out.

b. The players dribble in any direction inside the circle. On a given signal, the players leave the soccer ball in the circle, sprint to the nearest touchline, and sprint back. While the players are sprinting, the coach removes one ball from the circle. The player who is left without a ball is knocked out of the game. This continues until there is one ball and two players; the first player to reach the ball wins.

SOCCER BALL THROW-OUT

Soccer ball throw-out is a popular game that improves goalkeeping techniques. It can be conditioned to suit the needs of any players. The goalkeeper may simply be asked to fall on the ball, or to do more advanced aggressive diving, timing, and shepherding. Skills required of field players can range from basic inside of the foot dribbling to more advanced creative dribbling, using different parts of the feet and upper body to beat an opponent.

The game demands little in the way of equipment and field space. The number of players participating can be as few as six or as many as eighteen.

SOCCER BALL THROW-OUT *Situation 1*

Age Group	Ten to twelve years.
Number of Players	Six to eighteen (two teams, forwards and backs).
Time	Fifteen minutes.
Layout of Playing Area	See Figure 12–14.
Equipment	Two size four soccer balls, four cones or sweat tops or two benches.
Method of Play	The coach places the benches at the top of the goal area box. The players are divided into forwards and backs. They stand at the top of the penalty-area and face their respective benches. Two goalkeepers kneel down, one in front of each bench, and face the team players. One player from each team dribbles the ball toward the goalkeeper and tries to score by dribbling past the goalkeeper and holding the ball against the bench with the feet. The goalkeeper tries to dive and smother the ball or push it away from the bench. A goal is scored if, in the coach's opinion, the ball carrier successfully dribbles the ball past the goalkeeper. The team that scores the most goals wins.

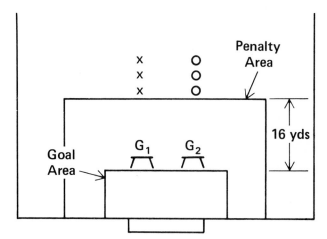

Figure 12–14. Layout for soccer ball throw-out situation 1.

$$\nearrow\!\!\searrow = \text{Bench}$$
x = Forwards
O = Backs
G = Goalkeeper

Rules

1. The ball carrier must not leave the target area.

2. The ball carrier may not kick the ball to score a goal.

3. The ball carrier is given ten to fifteen seconds in which to score.

4. The goalkeeper must kneel, except when diving for the ball.

Conditions Imposed on Players

1. The team players must try to control the ball while they dribble. They must use the inside of the feet.

2. The goalkeeper must try to dive sideways. Once he or she has the ball, the goalie rolls over and faces the bench.

Effect of Game

It improves the goalkeeper's timing, confidence, and diving technique. It also improves the field players' dribbling technique and awareness of time and space.

Suggestions

a. See Figure 12–15. X_2 and O_2 stand half the distance between the benches and the other team players. Their legs are spread apart, and they face the front of the penalty-area. X_1 and O_1 must dribble and play the ball through the legs of players X_2 and O_2 before they can try to score as in situation one. The goalkeeper may leave the bench to dive and smother the ball before possession can be regained by X_1 and O_1.

b. See Figure 12–16. The players sit around the top of the goal area and in

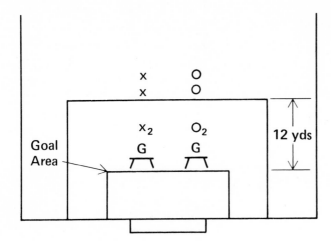

Figure 12–15. Layout for soccer ball throw-out situation 1.

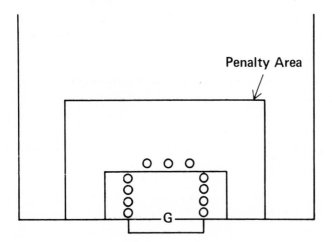

Figure 12–16. Layout for soccer ball throw-out situation 1.

front of the goalpost. They are assigned numbers. The goalkeeper kneels on the goal line facing the players. The players sit and pass the ball around the grid with their feet. The coach calls out one of the assigned numbers. That player jumps up, collects the ball with the feet, and tries to dribble the ball over the goal line and between the posts. The goalkeeper tries to smother the ball or push it away from the goal. All players' numbers must be called.

SOCCER BALL THROW-OUT *Situation 2*

Age Group	Thirteen to fifteen years.
Number of Players	Six to eighteen players (two teams, forwards and backs).
Time	Fifteen minutes.
Layout of Playing Area	See Figure 12–17.
Equipment	Two size five soccer balls.
Method of Play	The coach divides the players into two teams of forwards and backs. The players line up on either side of the halfway line and face the center circle. Two goalkeepers sit and face the team players, their feet touching the circle. Players X_1 and O_1 try to dribble their balls around the center circle line to the opposite side. The moment the balls are played, the goalkeepers jump up and try to dive and smother the balls or push them away from X_1 or O_1. A goal is scored every time a ball carrier succeeds in dribbling around the half circle. A player is eliminated if a goalkeeper smothers or pushes the ball away from the player's feet and the center circle line.
Rules	1. The players must attempt to dribble the ball on the line at all times.

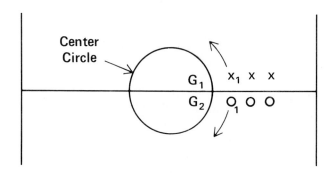

Figure 12–17. Layout for soccer ball throw-out situation 2.

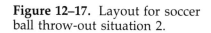

X = Forwards
O = Back
G = Goalkeeper

2. Players are eliminated if, in the coach's opinion, they wander away or lose control of the ball.

3. The goalkeepers must remain seated between saves or goals.

4. The ball carrier must not turn back at any time.

Conditions Imposed on Players

1. The team players must attempt to dribble the ball with the inside of the feet.

2. The goalkeepers must attempt to dive sideways to smother the ball.

Effect of Game

It improves the goalkeepers' confidence, speed off the mark, and diving technique. It also improves the field players' dribbling technique.

Suggestions

a. The goalkeepers lie flat on their stomachs or backs instead of sitting.

b. Ball carriers X_1 and O_2 drag the ball (with backs to the goalkeepers) around the circle.

SOCCER BALL THROW-OUT *Situation 3*

Age Group

Sixteen to eighteen years.

Number of Players

Six to eighteen players.

Time

Fifteen minutes.

Layout of Playing Area

See Figure 12–18.

Equipment

One size five soccer ball per player.

Method of Play

The team players stand in the center circle with balls at their feet. The goalkeepers stand outside the circle. Play commences when the players within the circle dribble the balls in any direction. The moment the players start to dribble the balls, the goalkeepers move into the circle and try to dive and smother the balls or throw them out of the center circle. Players are eliminated from the game if their balls are smothered, pushed, or thrown out of the circle. The last player dribbling the ball within the circle wins.

Rules

1. The ball carriers must stay within the center circle or they will be eliminated.

2. The goalkeeper must not kick the ball away from the ball carrier's feet and out of the circle.

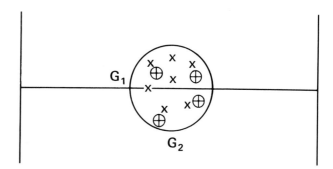

Figure 12–18. Layout for soccer ball throw-out situation 3.

x = Team Players
⊕ = Ball
G = Goalkeeper

Conditions Imposed on Players

1. The goalkeepers must dive sideways to smother the ball or push it away.
2. The ball carriers must try to dribble the ball with the inside and outside of the feet.
3. The ball carriers must try to move in all directions.

Effect of Game

It improves the goalkeepers' confidence, timing, and diving technique. It also improves the field players' awareness of time and space, ability to change pace, and dribbling technique.

Suggestions

a. If there are not enough soccer balls for all the players, the remaining players may move within the center circle and take the balls that become available when other players are eliminated from the game.
b. The goalkeepers compete for the greatest number of saves or balls thrown out of the circle.

CHAPTER THIRTEEN

Tactical Games for Creating Movement On and Off the Ball

Almost every novice soccer player wants to be where the action is. Kicking the ball leaves the player with a feeling of satisfaction and accomplishment. While a player is being introduced to soccer, his or her understanding of the game's scope will be limited. Movement on and off the ball, a sense of direction, team work, and even scoring goals are tactics beyond the beginner's comprehension.

Players who want to be near the ball and have a chance to kick it create a situation similar to that of bees swarming around a honey pot. Although the coach's screams and gestures indicate that he or she is trying to discourage this type of play, such advice falls on deaf ears. Twenty pairs of hands and feet will continue to push, shove, and kick with reckless abandon for what appears to be an eternity, only to explode and begin once again in another part of the fields.

Tactical games for creating movement on and off the ball develop the arts of isolating an opponent and creating space so that team players have room to dribble or pass the ball. The games presented in this chapter will gradually improve the player's awareness of time and space, and deepen his or her understanding of principles of attack. Once this hurdle has been overcome, the American soccer player will truly have come of age and will be able to stand tall in international competition.

These games are popular with all age groups. They require little in the way of equipment and supervision. Games should be selected that will counteract weaknesses observed by the coach during match play.

MOVEMENT ON THE BALL—GAMES USING TWO GOALS

MOVEMENT ON THE BALL *Situation 1*

Age Group	Ten to twelve years.
Number of Players	Eight to eighteen players (one versus one).
Time	Twenty-five seconds per pair, per stint.
Layout of Playing Area	See Figure 13–1.
Equipment	One size four soccer ball, cones, sweat tops, flags, and/or benches.

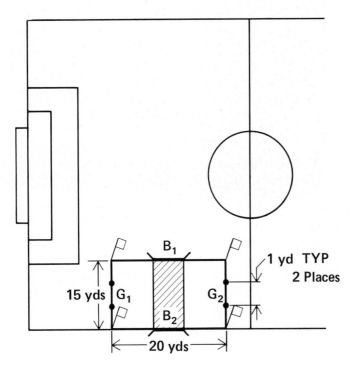

Figure 13–1. Movement on the ball, situation 1 (1 vs. 1): layout of playing area.

Method of
Play

The coach places grid markers and benches in position. The players are divided into two teams, and players on each team are numbered consecutively, beginning in each case with one. The two teams stand behind their respective benches, B_1 and B_2. The coach drops a ball and, at the same time, calls out one of the assigned numbers. The player whose number is called immediately runs toward the ball, tries to win possession, and dribbles it through either one of the goals, G_1 or G_2.

Rules

1. Players work for twenty-five seconds, no matter how many goals are scored in this time period.
2. Goals may be scored from the front or back of the goal.
3. The team that scores the highest number of goals wins.

Effect of
Game

The positioning of goals G_1 and G_2 encourages the player in possession of the ball to move laterally away from the bench area. Practicing lateral movement on the ball will help the players understand the importance of pulling central defenders out of position. They will realize that this creates space in which they or supporting players can carry or receive the ball. This will also improve the players' dribbling and tackling techniques.

Suggestions

a. The coach calls out a mixed pair of numbers; for example, one and five.

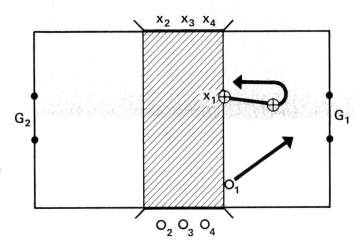

Figure 13–2. Movement on the ball, situation 1 (1 vs. 1): sample game.

O_1 = Defensive Player
x_1 = Ball Carrier
$\oplus$ = Soccer Ball
$\longrightarrow$ = Direction Players are Moving

This gives all of the players the opportunity to play against one another.

b. The players are divided into forwards and backs.

Sample Game Young players respond with enthusiasm to fake or trick plays that make their opponent go in the wrong direction. (See Figure 13–2.) Player X_1 gains possession of the ball in a central position, and immediately fakes a dribble toward goal G_1. The moment player O_1 races to protect the goal, player X_1 spins off in the opposite direction toward goal G_2.

MOVEMENT ON THE BALL *Situation 2*

Age group Thirteen to fifteen years.

Number of Players Eight to eighteen players.

Time Ten to fifteen seconds per run.

Layout of Playing Area See Figure 13–3.

Equipment One size five soccer ball for every two players; flags, cones, or sweat tops.

Method of Play The coach places the markers so that they form a rectangular grid. The players are paired off. They face each other from opposite sides of a grid.

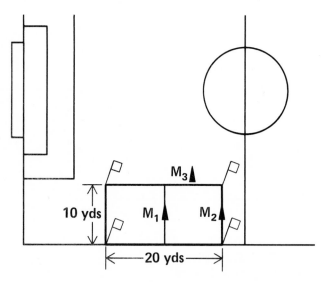

Figure 13–3. Movement on the ball, situation 2 (1 vs. 1): layout of playing area.

10 yds

M_3 M_1 M_2

◁— 20 yds —▷

◸ = Grid Markers
▲ = Game Markers

One player has a ball at the feet. Play commences when this player dribbles with good movement on the ball toward marker M_1, M_2, or M_3. The moment the ball carrier moves, the defender leaves marker M_3 to challenge and tackle the ball carrier. The defender tries to prevent the ball carrier from tagging the marker M_1, M_2, or M_3 for a score. The ball carrier is allowed three chances to score, each lasting ten to fifteen seconds. The player accumulating the highest number of goals wins.

Rules

1. The defending player must not leave the marker until the ball carrier touches the ball.
2. If the defensive player gets the ball away from the ball carrier, the game is restarted with the players back in their original positions.
3. The same marker may be tagged more than once.
4. The ball must be held on or against the markers with the feet for a count of two before a goal can be scored.

Effect of Game

It teaches the players how to isolate and draw a central defender out of position. It also improves the players' dribbling technique and ability to change the playing pace.

Suggestions

a. The defender must sit down at marker M_3 at every restart.
b. To encourage good movement on the ball, increase the number of goals to two for tagging marker M_1 or M_2 and five for tagging M_3. (See Figure 13–4.)

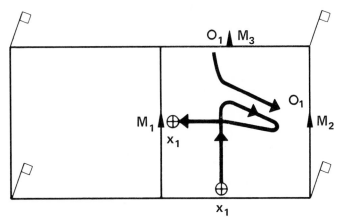

Figure 13–4. Movement on the ball, situation 2 (1 vs. 1): sample game.

O_1 = Defensive Player
x_1 = Ball Carrier
$\oplus$ = Soccer Ball
▲ = Goals
➡ = Direction Players Are Moving

Sample Game   Player X_1 dribbles the ball at speed toward defender O_1 and marker M_3. At the right moment, player X_1 spins off and dribbles the ball toward marker M_2. Defender O_1 immediately pursues X_1 to prevent a score. Having gained good body position on player O_1, player X_1 spins off once again and dribbles back toward marker M_3. Meanwhile, player O_1 tries to recover. Player X_1 now realizes that a move toward marker M_1 offers time and space for an easy score, since defender O_1 is completely out of position.

MOVEMENT ON THE BALL *Situation 3*

Age Group   Sixteen to eighteen years.

Number of Players   Eight to eighteen players.

Time   Thirty-five seconds.

Layout of Playing Area   See Figure 13–5.

Equipment   Three size five soccer balls; cones, flags, or sweat tops.

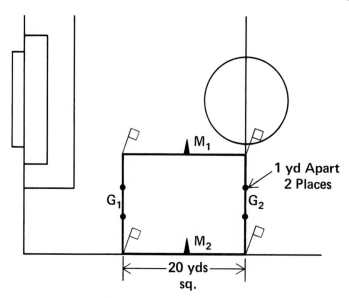

Figure 13–5. Movement on the ball, situation 3 (1 vs. 1): layout of playing area.

Method of
Play

The coach places the markers in position to form a grid. The players are paired off into forwards and backs. They stand behind markers M_1 and M_2. The coach decides which team will start the game, and places at least three balls at this team's marker. The first ball carrier dribbles with good movement on the ball from his or her marker toward goal G_1 or G_2. This player wants to score by dribbling the ball through the goal. As soon as the ball carrier moves, the defending player challenges. Whenever possible, the defending player tackles the ball away from the ball carrier to prevent a goal from being scored. The ball carrier must try to score as many goals as possible in thirty-five seconds. If the ball carrier scores a goal or loses possession of the ball, the procedure begins again from starting position. The ball is given to the other team when each player has completed two runs of thirty-five seconds each.

Rules

1. Both players must be at their respective markers before the game can restart.

2. The ball must stay within the boundary of the grid.

3. A ball retriever is placed behind G_1 and G_2.

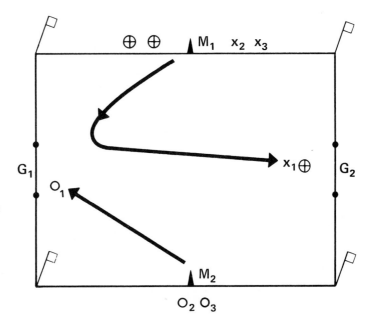

Figure 13–6. Movement on the ball, situation 3 (1 vs. 1): sample game.

O_1 = Defensive Player
x_1 = Ball Carrier
⊕⊕ = Soccer Balls
→ = Direction Players are Moving

Effect of Game	It improves the players' understanding of movement on the ball and time and space restraints in match-related conditions. It also improves the players' dribbling technique and ability to change the pace of play.
Suggestions	a. The ball carrier must dribble the ball with the weak foot.
	b. The goalkeeper can participate and put his or her diving skills to good use.
Sample Game	See Figure 13–6. Player X_1 has the ball and attacks in the direction of goal G_1. Player X_1 hopes to laterally move defending player O_1 out of a central position. Player O_1 reacts by trying to get between player X_1 and goal G_1. Player X_1 calmly cuts back inside of player O_1 toward goal G_2.

MOVEMENT ON AND OFF THE BALL USING TWO GOALS

MOVEMENT ON AND OFF THE BALL USING TWO GOALS *Situation 1*

Age Group	Ten to twelve years.
Number of Players	Six to eighteen players.
Time	Twenty-five seconds.
Layout of Playing Area	See Figure 13–7.
Equipment	One size four soccer ball; cones, flags, or sweat tops; benches.
Method of Play	The coach places markers M_1 and M_2 and goals G_1 and G_2 in position to form a grid. The players are divided into groups of three. They stand at their respective markers M_1, M_2, and M_3. Play commences when the player at marker M_3 dribbles the ball toward one of the goals, supported by a player from marker M_2. The moment the ball is dribbled into the grid, a defending player from marker M_1 races toward the goal to challenge or tackle the ball carrier and prevent a goal from being scored. With good movement on and off the ball, offensive players try to score a goal by holding the ball against the bench with their feet. Play continues for twenty-five seconds, no matter how many goals are scored. After twenty-five seconds, the players rotate: M_3 to M_1, M_1 to M_2, M_2 to M_3.
Rules	1. The supporting player must be in the opposite zone at all times.

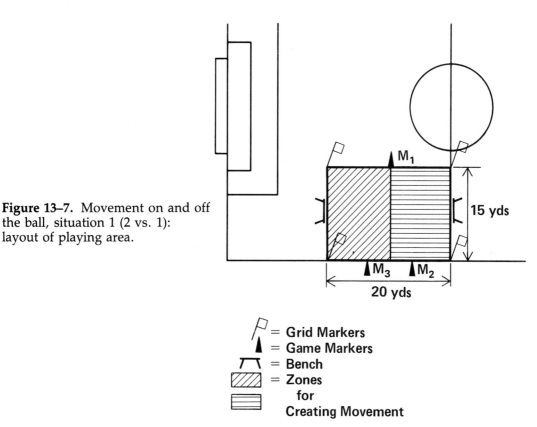

Figure 13–7. Movement on and off the ball, situation 1 (2 vs. 1): layout of playing area.

2. The ball carrier must hold the ball against the bench with the foot or dribble the ball through the goal before a goal is scored.

3. If the defender wins the ball or pushes it away from the ball carrier, the ball is immediately given back.

Effect of Game   It improves the players' understanding of movement on and off the ball; support in attack; and time and space. It also improves players' dribbling and passing techniques.

Suggestion   Right after the ball carrier dribbles the ball into the grid, the supporting player must sprint around the perimeter of the square before a two on one situation can be created. The ball carrier screens the ball until he or she has support.

Sample Game   See Figure 13–8. Player X_1 dribbles the ball into zone two to attack goal G_2. Defending player O_1 immediately gets goalside of ball carrier X_1, in order to prevent a goal from being scored. At this moment, supporting

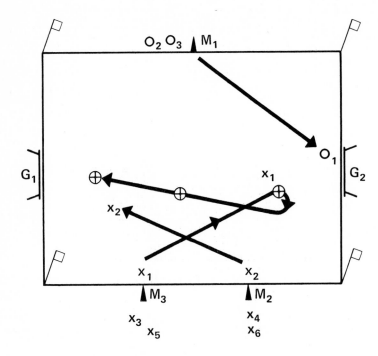

Figure 13–8. Movement on and off the ball, situation 1 (2 vs. 1): sample game.

O₁ = Defensive Player
x₁ = Ball Carrier
x₂ = Supporting Player
⊕→ = Direction of the Ball
→ = Direction Players Are Moving

player X_2 moves into zone one and calls for the ball. Player X_1 responds by spinning away from defending player O_1 and passing a lead ball to player X_2. X_2 scores in goal G_1.

MOVEMENT ON AND OFF THE BALL USING TWO GOALS *Situation 2*

Age Group	Thirteen to fifteen years.
Number of Players	Three to eighteen players (two versus one).
Time	Twelve minutes.
Layout of Playing Area	See Figure 13–9.
Equipment	One size five soccer ball for every three players; cones, flags, or sweat tops.

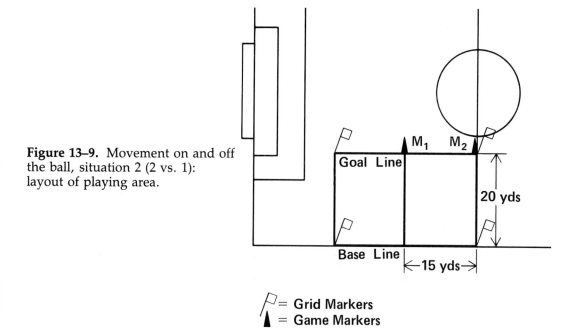

Figure 13–9. Movement on and off the ball, situation 2 (2 vs. 1): layout of playing area.

= Grid Markers
= Game Markers

Method of Play

The coach places the markers on the field to form a grid. The players are divided into groups of three. They stand in their respective corners of the grid. One of the baseline players dribbles the ball into the grid to attack the goal line. As soon as this ball carrier dribbles the ball into the grid, the defender at marker M_2 challenges to prevent a goal from being scored. The supporting offensive player at marker M_1 moves into the grid. This creates a two on one situation with the ball carrier. Together, with good movement on and off the ball, they try to score by dribbling the ball over the goal line. Each offensive pair has three chances to score. Roles are then exchanged.

Rules

1. Either offensive player may dribble the ball over the goal line to score a goal.

2. Offsides applies.

3. Every time a goal is scored or there is a breakdown in play, the game is restarted.

Effect of Game

It improves the players' understanding of movement on and off the ball; attack; and time and space. It also improves the players' dribbling and passing techniques.

Suggestions

a. The ball carrier and the supporting player leave from the baseline.

b. All three players stand on the baseline.

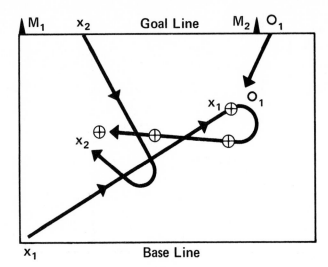

Figure 13–10. Movement on and off the ball, situation 2 (2 vs. 1): sample game.

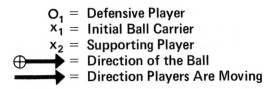

O_1 = Defensive Player
x_1 = Initial Ball Carrier
x_2 = Supporting Player
⊕➡ = Direction of the Ball
➡ = Direction Players Are Moving

c. The ball carrier stands in one corner, the defender stands in a central position, and the supporting offensive player sits in the other corner. The ball carrier tries to dribble the ball over the goal line while being challenged by the defender. The supporting player must jump up and support the ball carrier.

Sample Game   See Figure 13–10. Player X_1 dribbles the ball diagonally across the grid to attack the right side of the goal line. Defending player O_1 moves out of central position in order to prevent X_1 from scoring. At this moment, supporting player X_2 races back to get in front of the goal and receive a pass from player X_1. Player X_2 is free to advance and calmly dribble the ball over the goal line.

MOVEMENT ON AND OFF THE BALL USING TWO GOALS *Situation 3*

Age Group   Sixteen to eighteen years.

Number of Players   Three to eighteen players (two versus one).

Time   Twelve minutes.

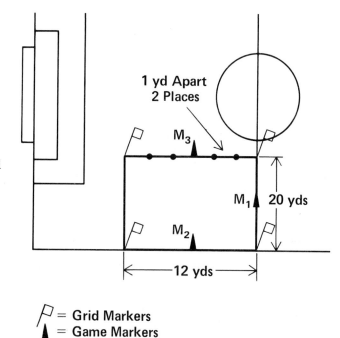

Figure 13–11. Movement on and off the ball, situation 3 (2 vs. 1): layout of playing area.

Layout of Playing Area	See Figure 13–11.
Equipment	One soccer ball per three players; cones, sweat tops, or flags.
Method of Play	The coach places grid markers M_1, M_2, and M_3, and goals G_1 and G_2 in position. The players are divided into groups of three. They stand in their respective grids at their particular marker. The ball carrier standing at M_2 passes the ball to the supporting player at M_1. Depending on the amount of pressure applied by the defending player from M_3, the supporting player has the option of dribbling or passing the ball back to the player at M_2. The player at M_2 can bring the ball into the grid and create a two on one situation. With good movement on and off the ball, they must try to score by dribbling the ball through goal G_1 or G_2. Players rotate so that each may experience all three positions.
Rules	1. The ball must be dribbled through the goals before a goal can be scored.
	2. The defender must exert heavy pressure.
	3. The player at M_2 may enter the grid only when the ball has been passed back to him or her.
	4. Every time a goal is scored or play breaks down, the game is restarted.

Effect of Game   It improves the players' understanding of movement on and off the ball; support in attack; and time and space. It also improves the players' dribbling and passing techniques.

Suggestions   a. The players play two versus one keep-away ball. The defensive player becomes an offensive player every time he or she wins the ball, or when five passes have been successfully completed by the offensive players.

b. The players stand in the center circle. They are assigned numbers. The even-numbered players are the offense, the odd-numbered players are the defense. The coach calls out any pair of even numbers and an odd number. When the offensive players have the ball, they play keep-away ball. When the defensive player has the ball, he or she screens the ball. Each group is given twenty-five to thirty-five seconds.

Sample Game   See Figure 13–12. Player X_1 passes the ball to supporting player X_2 in order to draw defending player O_1 away from a central position. Because of heavy pressure from defending player O_1, X_2 passes the ball back to X_1. This creates a two on one situation. Player X_1 attacks the same area of the grid in order to isolate defending player O_1. Player X_2, aware of the space

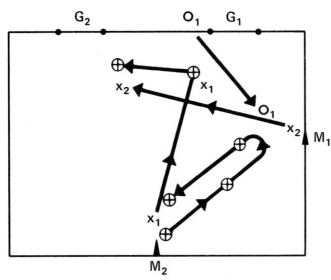

Figure 13–12. Movement on and off the ball, situation 3 (2 vs. 1): sample game.

O_1 = Defensive Player
X_1 = Offensive Player Starts the Game
X_2 = Supporting Player
⊕⟶ = Direction of the Ball
⟶ = Direction Players Are Moving

created on the left side of the grid, sprints into it, hoping to receive a pass or draw the defender away from ball carrier X_1. X_1 passes the ball to supporting player X_2. X_2 dribbles the ball through goal G_2.

MOVEMENT ON AND OFF THE BALL—GAMES USING THREE GOALS

MOVEMENT ON AND OFF THE BALL USING THREE GOALS *Situation 1*

Age Group	Ten to twelve years.
Number of Players	Five to twenty (three versus two).
Time	Twelve minutes.
Layout of Playing Area	See Figure 13–13.
Equipment	One size four soccer ball; flags, cones, or sweat tops.
Method of Play	The coach places markers M_1, M_2, and M_3 and goals G_1, G_2, and G_3 in position. The players are divided into groups of five. Then, the groups are subdivided, with three offensive and two defensive players in each group. The players stand at their respective markers. The player at M_3 dribbles the ball toward any unprotected goal, hoping to draw defending players out of position. The defending player closest to the unprotected goal moves quickly to protect the goal and prevent a score. The ball carrier must now try to bring in the other supporting offensive players and create

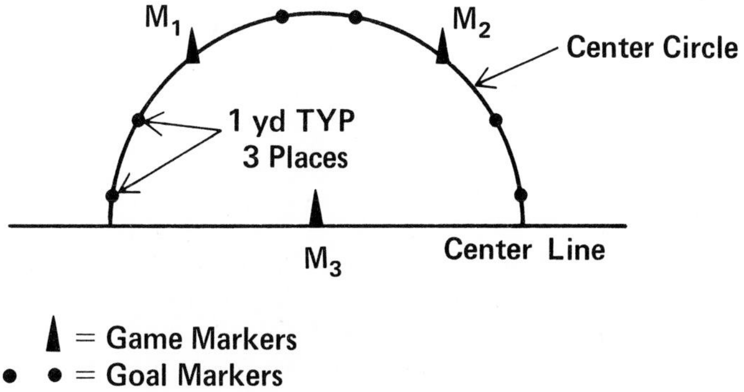

Figure 13–13. Movement on and off the ball, situation 1 (3 vs. 2).

a three on two situation. With good movement on and off the ball, these three players try to score in one of the three goals. The defending players try to prevent goals from being scored by using good tackling, marking, and covering techniques. Each time a goal is scored, the players rotate.

Rules

1. Player X_1 must attack the empty goal to start the game.
2. Defensive players only move around the perimeter of the circle.
3. Supporting offensive players must remain at their markers on the perimeter of the circle until they receive a pass.
4. The ball carrier may score goals by dribbling the ball out of the circle through goal G_1, G_2, or G_3.

Effect of Game

It improves the players' understanding of movement on and off the ball, depth in attack; and time and space. It also improves the players' dribbling and passing techniques.

Suggestion

Supporting offensive players may interchange positions around the perimeter of the circle.

Sample Game

See Figure 13–14. Player X_1 has the ball at the feet and dribbles it toward empty goal G_1. Player O_1 challenges player X_1. Supporting defending player O_2 moves into a position which covers both goals G_2 and G_3. The ball carrier X_1 passes the ball to supporting offensive player X_2. X_2 is immediately under pressure from defending player O_2. Player X_2 quickly passes the ball to supporting offensive player X_3, at empty goal G_3. X_3 dribbles the ball through G_3.

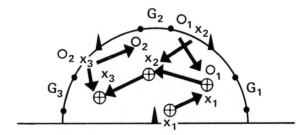

Figure 13–14.

O_1 = Defensive Player Challenging for the Ball
O_2 = Supporting Defensive Player
x_1 = Offensive Player Starts the Play
x_2, x_3 = Supporting Offensive Players
⊕→ = Direction of the Ball
→ = Direction Players Are Moving

MOVEMENT ON AND OFF THE BALL USING THREE GOALS *Situation 2*

Age Group   Thirteen to fifteen years.

Number of   Five through twenty.
Players

Time   Twelve minutes.

Layout of   See Figure 13–15.
Playing Area

Equipment   One size five soccer ball; flags, cones, or sweat tops.

Method of   The coach places the grid markers and goals G_1, G_2, and G_3 in position.
Play   The players are divided into groups of five. Within the groups, they are
                       subdivided into three offensive and two defensive players. One of the
                       offensive players dribbles the ball in any direction within the grid. Sup-
                       porting players, with good movement off the ball, either move into spaces
                       that will draw defenders out of position so that the ball carrier can score,
                       or move into spaces where they can receive a pass and score. The ball may
                       be dribbled through the goal in any direction.

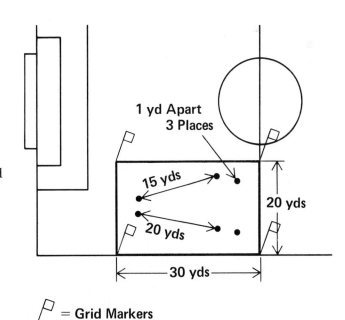

Figure 13–15. Movement on and
off the ball, situation 2 (3 vs. 2).

Rules

1. A goal may be scored by dribbling the ball through the back or the front of a goal.

2. Players change positions if there is a passing error, the ball is lost in a tackle, or the ball is passed out of the grid.

Effect of Game

It improves the players' understanding of movement on and off the ball; depth in attack; time and space. It also improves the players' dribbling and passing techniques.

Suggestions

a. If the defensive pair gains possession of the ball, they play keep-away. If they maintain possession of the ball for ten seconds or put together three passes, they are awarded one goal.

b. If the offensive trio loses possession of the ball, or a pass goes outside the grid, the three players run one lap of the grid's perimeter. The last two players back replace the defensive pair.

Sample Game

See Figure 13–16. Player X_1 possesses the ball and is supported by players X_2 and X_3. Defending players O_1 and O_2 are within range of all three offensive players. However, they are in a straight line, and there is open space in a central position, in front of goal G_2. Ball carrier X_1 passes the ball to supporting player X_2, who immediately plays a through ball toward goal G_2. Supporting player X_3 sprints behind defensive players O_1 and O_2 and scores.

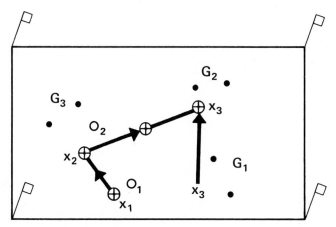

Figure 13–16.

O_1 = Defensive Player Challenging for the Ball
O_2 = Supporting Defensive Player
X_1 = Offensive Player Starts the Game
X_2, X_3 = Supporting Offensive Players
⊕⟶ = Direction of the Ball
⟶ = Direction Players Are Moving

MOVEMENT ON AND OFF THE BALL USING THREE GOALS *Situation 3*

Age Group	Sixteen to eighteen years.
Number of Players	Five to twenty players (three versus two).
Time	Twelve minutes.
Layout of Playing Area	See Figure 13–17.
Equipment	One size five soccer ball per group; flags, cones, or sweat tops.
Method of Play	The coach places grid markers and goals G_1, G_2, and G_3 in position. The players are divided into groups of five, and then subdivided within each group into three offensive and two defending players. One of the offensive players takes a throw-in, propelling the ball to one of the supporting player's feet. The moment the ball is controlled, the defenders challenge for it. The supporting offensive players, with good movement on and off the ball, try to create situations whereby they can receive or dribble the ball and then score. Every time a goal is scored or there is a breakdown

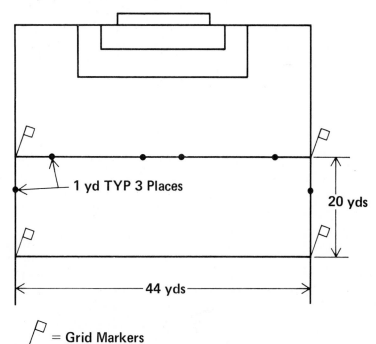

Figure 13–17. Movement on and off the ball, situation 3 (3 vs. 3).

1 yd TYP 3 Places

20 yds

44 yds

$\nearrow$ = Grid Markers

• • = Goal Markers

in play, players rotate. The game is restarted with a throw-in from outside the grid.

Rules   A goal is scored every time the ball is dribbled through one of the goals.

Effect of Game   It improves the players' understanding of movement on and off the ball; depth in attack; time and space. It also improves the players' dribbling, passing, and ball control techniques.

Suggestions

a. From the throw-in, the ball must be headed back to the thrower at the start or restart of the game.

b. Should the defending players intercept or win the ball in a tackle, they must attempt to dribble the ball out of the grid.

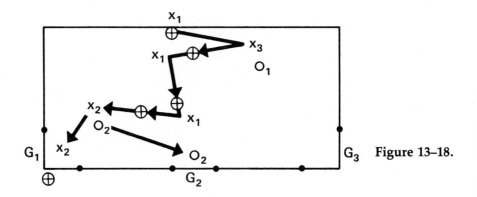

Figure 13–18.

O_1, O_2 = Defensive Players
X_1 = Offensive Player Starts the Play
X_2, X_3 = Supporting Offensive Players
⊕→ = Direction of the Ball
→ = Direction Players Are Moving

Sample Game   See Figure 13–18. Player X_1 has the ball and makes a throw-in to the feet of player X_3. Player X_3 controls the ball with the sole of the foot, and quickly passes it back to X_1 because of pressure exerted by defending player O_1. Player X_1 controls the ball and dribbles at speed in front of goal G_2. Defending player O_2 moves to prevent a goal from being scored, leaving player X_2 unmarked. Ball carrier X_1, realizing that his or her time and space has been restricted, passes the ball to supporting player X_2. X_2 controls the ball and dribbles it through goal G_1 for a score.

MOVEMENT ON AND OFF THE BALL—GAMES USING FOUR GOALS

MOVEMENT ON AND OFF THE BALL USING FOUR GOALS *Situation 1*

Age Group   Ten to twelve years.

Number of Players   Six to eighteen players (four versus two).

Time   Twelve minutes.

Layout of Playing Area   See Figure 13–19.

Equipment   One size four soccer ball per group; flags, cones, sweat tops, or benches.

Method of Play   The coach places the grid markers and goals G_1, G_2, G_3, and G_4 into position. The players are divided into groups of seven, and then subdivided into four offensive and three defensive players. One of the offensive team players side foot passes the ball into the grid to a supporting player. With good movement on and off the ball, the offensive players try to create

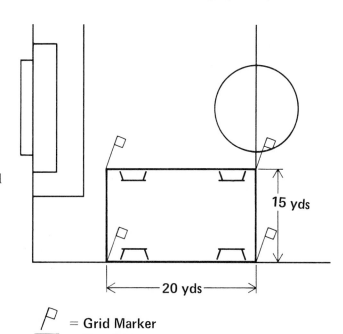

Figure 13–19. Movement on and off the ball, situation 1 (4 vs. 3).

15 yds

20 yds

= Grid Marker

= Benches

goal-scoring situations. The defending pair tries to prevent goals from being scored. Defending players rotate and the game is restarted every time a goal is scored, a player loses possession of the ball in a tackle, or an errant pass goes outside of the grid.

Rules

1. Play commences when one of the offensive players side foot passes the ball into the grid to one of the supporting players.

2. Goals are scored either by holding the ball with the foot against the bench, or by dribbling the ball through the goal.

Effect of Game

It improves the players' understanding of movement on and off the ball; depth in attack; and time and space. It also improves the players' dribbling and passing techniques.

Suggestions

a. Play walking soccer.

b. If the defending pair gains possession of the ball, the four offensive players pair off for a horse and jockey race around the perimeter of the grid. The last pair back becomes the new set of defenders.

Sample Game

See Figure 13–20. Player X_3 stands outside the grid with a ball at the feet. Supporting players X_1 and X_2 isolate defending players O_1 and O_2 at goals

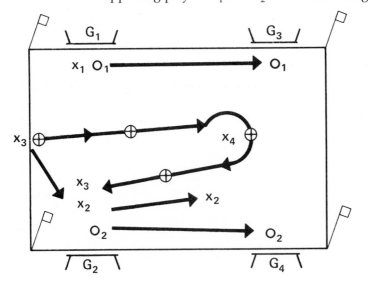

Figure 13–20.

O_1, O_2 = Defensive Players
X_3 = Offensive Player Starts the Game
X_1, X_2, X_4 = Supporting Offensive Players
⊕——▶ = Direction of the Ball
——▶ = Direction Players Are Moving

G_1 and G_2. This creates space for player X_1 to side foot pass the ball to supporting player X_4. Player X_4 controls the ball and dribbles it toward goal G_3. Defending player O_1 tries to prevent the goal from being scored. At this moment, player X_2 moves quickly toward goal G_4, drawing defending player O_2 with him or her. This leaves space in front of goal G_2. Ball carrier X_4 side foot passes the ball back to supporting player X_3. X_3 scores at goal G_2.

MOVEMENT ON AND OFF THE BALL USING FOUR GOALS *Situation 2*

Age Group   Thirteen to fifteen years.

Number of   Seven to twenty-one players (four versus three).
Players

Time   Fifteen minutes.

Layout of   See Figure 13–21.
Playing Area

Equipment   One size five soccer ball per group of seven players; flags, cones, sweat
                   tops, or benches.

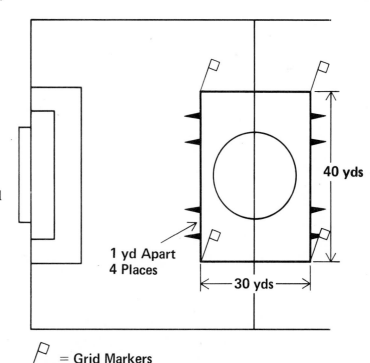

Figure 13–21. Movement on and off the ball, situation 2 (4 vs. 3).

1 yd Apart
4 Places

40 yds

← 30 yds →

= Grid Markers
= Goal Markers

*Method of
Play*

The coach places the grid markers and goals G_1, G_2, G_3, and G_4 into position. The players are divided into groups of seven, then subdivided into four offensive players and three defensive players. One of the offensive team players side foot passes the ball into the grid to one of the supporting players. With good movement on and off the ball, the offensive players try to create goal-scoring situations. The defending trio will try to prevent goals. After every goal, players rotate and the game is restarted with a side foot pass from outside the grid.

Rules

1. A goal is scored every time the ball is dribbled through any of the goals.
2. The ball must be dribbled or passed across the center line before the offensive team can change the direction of the play from one pair of goals, G_1 and G_2, to the other pair, G_3 and G_4.
3. The defending players can score if, upon an interception or upon winning the ball in a tackle: (a) they can interpass the ball into the center circle; or (b) one of the players can dribble the ball into the center circle.

*Effect of
Game*

It improves the players' understanding of movement on and off the ball; depth in attack; and time and space. It also improves the players' dribbling and passing techniques.

Suggestions

a. The offensive team must score in one pair of goals, G_1 and G_2 or G_3 and G_4, before they can attack the other pair.

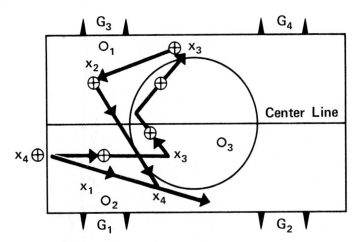

Figure 13–22.

O_1, O_2, O_3 = Defensive Players
x_4 = Offensive Player Starts the Game
x_1, x_2, x_3 = Supporting Offensive Players
⊕——▶ = Direction of the Ball
——▶ = Direction Players Are Moving

b. If the defensive trio intercepts the ball, they will play keep-away. For every successful pass they complete, the original four offensive players must take one lap around the grid. The last three to finish become the new defenders.

Sample Game   See Figure 13–22. Player X_4 stands outside the grid with a ball at the feet. Supporting players X_1 and X_2 have isolated defending players O_1 and O_2 at goals G_3 and G_1. Supporting player X_3 is in a central, deep position, with space in front of him or her, and is marked by defending player O_3. Player X_4 side foot passes the ball to supporting player X_3. Player X_3 dribbles the ball across the center line while being pursued by, and drawing out of position, central defender O_3. X_3 now passes the ball to supporting player X_2. X_2 passes the ball toward goal G_2, for supporting player X_4. X_4 moves into the space vacated by supporting player X_3 and defender O_3. Player X_4 has enough time and space to control the ball and score.

MOVEMENT ON AND OFF THE BALL USING FOUR GOALS *Situation 3*

Age Group   Sixteen to eighteen years.

Number of Players   Seven to twenty-one players (four versus three).

Time   Fifteen to twenty minutes (three minutes per group).

Layout of Playing Area   See Figure 13–23.

Equipment   Four size five soccer balls per group; flags, cones, or sweat tops.

Method of Play   The coach places the grid zone and goals markers G_1, G_2, G_3, and G_4 in position. The players are divided into groups of seven, and then subdivided into four offensive players and three defensive players. One of the offensive players dribbles or passes the ball into the grid. The four offensive players, with good movement on and off the ball, try to create the most favorable goal-scoring situation they can in the allowed time of three minutes. The defensive players sprint away from the goal line and try to prevent goals from being scored. The offensive unit scoring the highest number of goals in three minutes wins.

Rules   1. Goals are scored when the ball is dribbled through the front of any of the four goals.

2. All players return to their original positions when a goal is scored, the ball is passed out of the grid, or the defensive team gains possession of the ball.

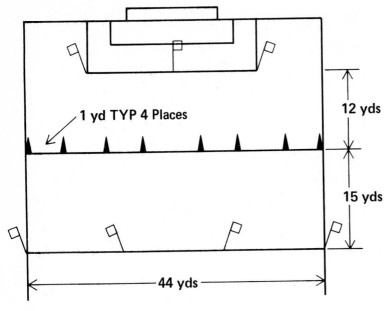

1 yd TYP 4 Places

12 yds

15 yds

Figure 13–23. Movement on and off the ball, situation 3 (4 vs. 3).

|← ——— **44 yds** ——— →|

= Player Starting Position
(All Equally Spaced)
= Goal Markers

3. Another ball is used every time players return to their original positions.

4. All players must be at their respective markers before the game can be restarted.

5. The same offensive player cannot restart the game unless groups change every three minutes.

6. Groups change every three minutes.

7. Game balls must be retrieved by a nonplayer and quickly placed behind appropriate marker.

Effect of Game   It improves the players' understanding of movement on and off the ball; depth in attack; time and space when under pressure. It also improves the players' dribbling and passing techniques.

Suggestions   a. Increase the goal size to four yards and introduce goalkeepers into the game.

b. Unknown to the defensive trio, the offensive players attempt to score the goals in sequence, going from G_1, to G_2, to G_3, and G_4.

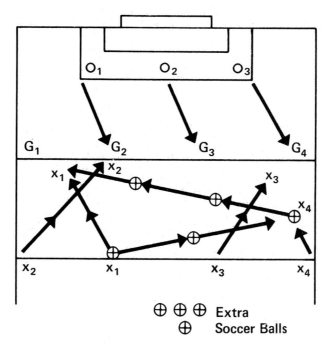

Figure 13–24.

O_1, O_2, O_3 = Defensive Players
x_1, x_2, x_3, x_4 = Offensive Players
$\oplus$➤ = Direction of the Ball
➤ = Direction Players Are Moving

Sample Game   See Figure 13–24. Player X_1 has the ball at the feet and starts the game with an instep pass to player X_4. X_4 controls the ball and moves in the direction of goal G_4, supported by player X_3. Defensive players O_2 and O_3 are committed to and isolated at goals G_3 and G_4. Defensive player O_1 is left to protect goals G_1 and G_2. X_4 passes the ball to supporting player X_2, who has moved in to attack and isolate defender O_1 at goal G_2. Offensive player X_2 controls the ball, spins off, and passes to supporting player X_1. X_1 has made a diagonal run into the space in front of goal G_1. Player X_1 has the time and space to control the ball and score a goal.

CHAPTER FOURTEEN

Soccer Fitness Exercises

Every sport has its own unique fitness requirements. A soccer game requires ninety minutes of physical and mental excellence from its players. Endurance, strength, mobility, and mental awareness make a good soccer player.

Soccer fitness emphasizes mobility because of the amount of running, jumping, and turning that is done during a game. The coach should teach players these skills during training sessions.

The twenty soccer fitness exercises presented in this chapter are a compilation of the most popular and respected exercises found in coaching manuals. These exercises will develop the player's flexibility and muscular strength. Stretching exercises have also been included. Stretching exercises should be done before and after training sessions. They should be done slowly in order to prevent muscle pulls and tears.

Exercises that develop general endurance have not been included in this chapter, since the best way to develop stamina is to play soccer. Many of the games presented in previous chapters should help the player build endurance. However, if the coach wants to include endurance training in the program, it is important that such training include (a) use of the soccer ball, and (b) situations that involve stopping, starting, twisting, turning, and jumping. Running laps around the soccer field is time consuming, boring, and will not help youngsters meet the high standards required of the American soccer player.

The following exercises should be implemented in the training program on a rotating basis. Each area of the body should be worked on during each session. The repetitions and times presented in this chapter are offered as a guide.

The following format is suggested for adapting the program to players of various ages.

1. Players sixteen to eighteen years old should be expected to achieve the maximum number of repetitions during the course of the season.
2. Intermediate players, thirteen to fifteen years old, should be expected to achieve at least two-thirds of the repetitions during the course of the season.
3. Junior players, ten to twelve years old, should be expected to achieve one-third of the repetitions during the course of the season.

It is important not to exceed these guidelines, for players should not become overtired. For the same reason, a cooling down period must follow every repetition. The players can use this time to do some stretching exercises.

The unconventional names given to these exercises are used solely to motivate players.

EXERCISE 1 *Irish Jig*

Number of Players	One to three players per soccer ball.
Number of Reps	Three.
Time	Thirty-five seconds per rep.
Method	The player places one foot on the soccer ball. On command, the player begins to rapidly alternate feet, placing first one and then the other on the ball. (See Figure 14–1.)
Effect of Exercise	Develops the calf muscles.
Suggestions	Players compete for the highest number of touches on the soccer ball in the allowed time. The players clap every time a foot touches the soccer ball.
Recovery Time	About three times the work rate.
Recovery Exercise	Hamstring stretch. The player rolls the soccer ball around the feet. (See Figure 14–2.)

Figure 14–1. Irish jig (feet on and off the soccer ball).

Figure 14–2. Hamstring stretch.

EXERCISE 2 *Push-ups on the Soccer Ball*

Number of Players	One player per soccer ball.
Number of Reps	Ten times; increase to thirty.
Time	Set own time.
Method	The player kneels with hands on the ball. The legs are extended back. On command, the player executes a push-up on the ball. The ball must be directly under the chest at all times. (See Figure 14–3.)
Effect of Exercise	Develops the back of the upper arms, the chest, and the shoulders.
Suggestion	The player holds a half arm bent push-up position for a count of seven seconds.
Recovery Time	About three times the work rate.
Recovery Exercise	Bilateral quadriceps stretch. The player kneels on the ground and sits back on the heels, ankles fully stretched. The hands are then placed as far back

Figure 14–3. Push-ups on the soccer ball.

as possible, keeping knees on the ground. Player returns to an upright position. Repeat ten times.

EXERCISE 3 *Jumping Over the Soccer Ball*

Number of Players	One player per soccer ball.
Number of Reps	Three.
Time	Thirty-five seconds per rep.
Method	The player stands beside the soccer ball. On command, the player begins to jump from one side of the ball to the other, making sure to concentrate on the soccer ball. (See Figure 14–4.)

Figure 14–4. Jumping over the soccer ball (side to side).

Figure 14–5. Flex and stretch (bilateral quadriceps, hamstrings, and calf muscles).

Effect of Exercise	Develops the calf and thigh muscles.
Suggestions	If a player experiences difficulty in maintaining continuous jumping, allow an intermediate jump on either side of the ball until the player can properly complete the exercise.
Recovery Time	Three times the work rate.
Recovery Exercise	Bilateral quadriceps, hamstrings, and calf muscles stretch. The player stands with the legs apart and rolls the ball around the feet in a large circle. The ball may also be passed through the legs to form a figure eight. (See Figure 14–5.)

EXERCISE 4 *Push-ups Over the Soccer Ball*

Number of Players	One player per soccer ball.
Number of Reps	Ten times; increase to thirty.
Time	Set own time.
Method	The player kneels on all fours. The soccer ball is directly underneath the stomach. The legs are extended back and the player holds a push-up po-

Figure 14–6. Push-ups over the soccer ball.

Figure 14–7. Groin stretch.

sition. On command, the player moves the trunk to the left of the soccer ball and lowers the chest to the ground. The player then pushes up, moves the trunk to the right of the soccer ball, and lowers the chest. Repeat. (See Figure 14–6.)

Effect of Exercise	Develops the back of the upper arms and shoulders.
Suggestion	The player holds a half arm bent push-up position for a count of seven seconds on each side of the soccer ball.
Recovery Time	Three times the work rate.
Recovery Exercise	Groin stretch. The player stands on one leg and raises the other leg, knee bent and turned out as far as possible. Repeat ten times. (See Figure 14–7.)

EXERCISE 5 *Tuck Jumps*

Number of Players	All players.
Number of Reps	Ten times; increase to thirty.
Time	Set own time.

Figure 14–8. Tuck jumps.

Method	On command, the player begins to continuously jump, bringing the knees high up into the chest. (See Figure 14–8.)
Effect of Exercise	Develops the calf, thigh, and abdomen muscles.
Suggestion	The players count off the repetitions in unison.
Recovery Time	Three times the work rate.
Recovery Exercise	Flex and stretch. The player stands with the legs apart. The ball is held out to the front, arms fully extended. The player moves the ball around the head, making large circles. Reverse direction.

EXERCISE 6 *Leg Curls*

Number of Players	One or two players per ball.
Number of Reps	Ten times; increase to thirty.
Time	Set own time.
Method	The player lies down, knees bent, soccer ball held lightly between the ankles, hands locked behind the head. On command, the player sits up and then returns to the original position. (See Figure 14–9.)

Figure 14–9. Leg curls.

Figure 14–10. Flex and stretch.

Effect of Exercise	Develops the abdomen muscles.
Recovery Time	Three times the work rate.
Recovery Exercise	The player lies on the back, arms stretched out to the sides. The player crosses the left leg over the right leg, and works it up to the right hand. If possible, the seat should remain flat on the ground. Repeat ten times. (See Figure 14–10.)

EXERCISE 7 *Jumping Over the Soccer Ball, Front to Back*

Number of Players	One player per ball.
Number of Reps	Three.
Time	Fifteen seconds; increase to thirty-five.
Method	The player stands with the soccer ball in front of the feet. On command, the player jumps over the ball and then jumps back, keeping the feet together at all times. (See Figure 14–11.)
Effect of Exercise	Develops calf muscles.
Suggestion	The players move to different locations to prevent wear and tear on the training area.

Figure 14–11. Jumping over the soccer ball (front to back).

Recovery Time	Three times the work rate.
Recovery Exercise	The player lies on the back, one leg raised slightly off of the ground. The player slowly rotates the ankle clockwise, then counterclockwise, ten times.

EXERCISE 8 *Swivel Hips*

Number of Players	One per soccer ball.
Number of Reps	Three.
Time	Fifteen seconds; increase to thirty-five.
Method	The player sits on the ground with the legs extended, the soccer ball held tightly between the ankles. The player raises the legs while holding the ball. Then he or she swings the legs to the right, at the same time swinging

Figure 14–12. Swivel hips. Flex.

Figure 14–13. Flex and stretch (figure eights around and through legs).

the extended arms to the left. On command, the player alternates position of legs and arms in a continuous motion. (See Figure 14–12.)

Effect of Exercise   Develops abdomen and lower back muscles.

Suggestion   This exercise is best performed to popular music or rhythm counting.

Recovery Time   Three times work rate.

Recovery Exercise   The player stands with legs apart and holds a ball in one hand. The ball is taken around the knees and through the legs, forming a figure eight. (See Figure 14–13.)

EXERCISE 9 *Squat Jump-Thrust*

Number of Players   All players.

Number of Reps   Three.

Time   Fifteen seconds; increase to thirty-five.

Method   The player squats. On command, the player jumps up, fully extending his or her body, and then returns to the original squatting position. (See Figure 14–14.)

Effect of Exercise   Primarily develops upper thigh muscles. It also activates other muscle groups.

Suggestion   Pair off players and have them compete for greatest number of squat jumps in the allotted time.

Figure 14–14. Squat jump-thrust.

Recovery Time   Three times work rate.

Recovery   Technique. Individual ball lifting, instep only. (See Figure 5–1 page 40).
Exercise

EXERCISE 10 *Pink Panther*

Number of   All players.
Players

Number of   Ten; increase to thirty.
Reps

Time   Set own time.

Method   The player sits. On command, the player raises legs to a fully extended
                   position, hands locked behind the neck. The player then brings one knee
                   in to touch the chest, keeping feet off the ground at all times. (See Figure
                   14–15.) The player repeats, alternating legs.

Effect of   Develops upper thigh and abdomen muscles.
Exercise

Suggestions   This particular exercise is best performed to the tune of the "Pink Panther"
                   or "Mickey Mouse." Also try speeding up or slowing down the beat.

Recovery Time   Three times work rate.

Figure 14–15. Pink panther.

Figure 14–16. Flex and stretch.

Recovery Exercise	Hamstring stretch. The player sits on the ground, legs fully extended, a ball placed near the hip. The ball is rolled by hand around the feet and back around the player. Repeat ten times. (See Figure 14–16.)

EXERCISE 11 *Leap Frog*

Number of Players	All players, paired off.
Number of Reps	Ten; increase to thirty (three sets each).
Time	Set own time.
Method	The players are paired off. One stands behind the other. (The back player is the jumper.) The front player has his or her legs about eighteen inches apart, body semi-bent, arms straight, and hands held firmly above the kneecap. On command, the back player leaps over the front player, then dives back through the front players legs and repeats the exercise. (See Figure 14–17.) Players change positions.
Effect of Exercise	Develops the jumping player's arm and shoulder muscles, and the bending player's calf and thigh muscles.
Suggestion	The players compete for the highest number of leaps in an allotted time.

Figure 14–17. Leap frog: over (top) and through legs.

Figure 14–18. Flexibility and stretch: overhead (top) and through legs (bottom).

Recovery Time   Three times work rate.

Recovery Exercise   Flex and stretch. Two players stand back to back, about a foot apart. One player takes a ball back over the head (as in a throw-in). The other player reaches back, grabs the ball, and passes it through the legs. The first player reaches back through the legs, grabs the ball, and repeats the process in a continuous motion. (See Figure 14–18.) Note: The distance between the players must be long enough to make the players stretch for the ball.

EXERCISE 12 *Twisting Push-ups*

Number of Players   All players are paired off.

Number of Reps   Ten; increase to twenty (three sets each).

Time   Set own time.

Method   One player sits on the ground. The other player kneels and lightly grips the first player's feet. On command, the sitting player twists to the left or right, does a push-up, and returns to the original position. The player then twists to the other side, performs another push-up, returns to the original position, and repeats. (See Figure 14–19.) Players change positions.

Figure 14–19. Twisting push-ups.

Figure 14–20. Flex and stretch (give and take).

Effect of Exercise	Develops arm and shoulder muscles.
Suggestion	The players chant in unison, one and two and three and four.
Recovery Time	Three times the work rate.
Recovery Exercise	Flex and stretch. Two players sit back to back, about two feet apart. One player holds a ball in the hands. The ball carrier twists and passes the ball to the other player. This player grabs the ball in both hands, takes it around the body, twists, and passes it back again. Repeat in continuous motion (See Figure 14–20.)

EXERCISE 13 *Tuck Jumps (over and under)*

Number of Players	All players are paired off.
Number of Reps	Ten; increase to thirty (three sets each).
Time	Set own time
Method	One player kneels on all fours. The other player stands beside the first player. On command, the standing player tuck jumps over the kneeling

Figure 14–21. Tuck jumps (over and under).

player. This player then crawls back underneath the kneeling player and repeats the exercise. (See Figure 14–21.) Players change positions.

Effect of Exercise	Develops calf and upper thigh muscles.
Suggestion	The players compete for the greatest number of tucks in the allotted time.
Recovery Time	Three times work rate.
Recovery Exercise	Technique. Individual soccer ball lifting with the thigh. (See Figure 5–8 page 47.)

EXERCISE 14 *Boxing the Partner's Feet*

Number of Players	All players are paired off.
Number of Reps	Three sets each.
Time	Ten seconds; increase to thirty-five.

Method   One player lies flat on his or her back, hands locked under the spine. The other player stands at this player's feet. On command, the player on the ground raises the feet as high as possible, fully extends them, and moves them in all directions. The standing player assumes a boxer's stance and tries to box the partner's feet. (See Figure 14–22.)

Figure 14–22. Boxing partner's feet.

Figure 14–23. Hamstring stretch.

Effect of Exercise	Develops abdomen, calf, and thigh muscles.
Recovery Time	Three times work rate.
Recovery Exercise	Stretch hamstrings. One player lightly holds the heel of the other player's right foot, the hands just below waist height. The player who is balanced on one foot slowly moves the head down to touch the knee of the raised leg. The player returns to an upright position. Repeat, changing legs. (See Figure 14–23.)

EXERCISE 15 *Horse and Jockey*

Number of Players	All players are paired off.
Number of Reps	Ten; increase to thirty (three sets each).
Time	Set own time.

Figure 14–24. Horse and jockey (toe raisers).

Method	One player stands behind the other. On command, the back player, or jockey, jumps on the front player's back. On command, the front player, or horse, raises up on the toes, holds, and then lowers. (See Figure 14–24.)
Effect of Exercise	Develops calf muscles.
Suggestion	The front player holds the raised position for a count of seven seconds.
Recovery Time	Three times work rate.
Recovery Exercise	Technique. Individual soccer ball lifting with the head. (See Figure 5–11 page 50.)

EXERCISE 16 *Two in a Boat*

Number of Players	All players are paired off.
Number of Reps	Fifteen; increase to thirty.
Time	Set own time.
Method	Players sit, feet to feet. On command, the players grasp each others hands or wrists and begin rocking back and forth. One player's legs will be semi-extended, and the other player's legs will be bent. (See Figure 14–25.)

Figure 14–25. Two in a boat. Flex and stretch.

Figure 14–26. Hamstring and groin stretch.

Effect of Exercise	Develops abdomen muscles.
Suggestion	The players chant "in-out," or sing "Row, Row, Row Your Boat."
Recovery Time	Three times work rate.
Recovery Exercise	Hamstring and groin stretch. Same movement as exercise fourteen, except that the player standing on one leg stands sideways beside the supporting player. (See Figure 14–26.)

EXERCISE 17 *Reach for the Sky*

Number of Players	All players are paired off.
Number of Reps	Ten; increase to twenty-five (three sets each).
Time	Set own time.
Method	One player kneels on all fours. The other player stands beside the kneeling player's feet. On command, the standing player lifts the kneeling player's legs so that they flank the standing player's waistline. The standing player locks the hands under and across the partner's thighs. On command, the standing player lifts up the partner, while the partner pushes himself or

Figure 14–27. Reach for the sky.

Figure 14–28. Flex and stretch.

herself upward from the push-up position, reaching for the sky. (See Figure 14–27.)

Effect of Exercise	Develops arm, shoulder and abdomen muscles.
Suggestion	Exercise can be done to the sea chanty "What Shall We Do with the Drunken Sailor?" using the chorus "Hooray, and up she rises."
Recovery Time	Three times work rate.

Recovery
Exercise

Flex and stretch. The players sit facing each other. The knees are bent, legs apart, feet touching. One player holds the ball in the hands, arms fully extended. This player then lies back on the ground, moving the ball as far back as possible over the head and resting it on the ground. In one motion, the player brings the ball back to the original position. The other player then stretches forward, takes the ball, and repeats the exercise. Repeat ten times each. (See Figure 14–28.)

EXERCISE 18 *The Seal Clap*

Number of
Players

All players are paired off.

Number of
Reps

Ten; increase to twenty-five (three sets each).

Time

Set own time.

Method

One player lies flat on the stomach, arms fully extended in front of the body. The other player kneels and holds the partner's ankles. On command, the player lying on the stomach lifts the upper body off the ground and claps hands. (See Figure 14–29.)

Effect of
Exercise

Develops abdomen muscles.

Figure 14–29. Seal clap.

Suggestion	The lying player clasps hands behind the neck.
Recovery Time	Three times work rate.
Recovery Exercise	Technique. In pairs, players pass and control the ball with the inside and outside of the foot. (See Figure 5–5 page 44.)

EXERCISE 19 *Tug of War*

Number of Players	All players are paired off.
Number of Reps	Three.
Time	Thirty-five seconds.
Method	Two players stand and face each other, the tips of their toes touching. On command, the players grip each other's wrists and begin tugging. (See Figure 14–30.)
Effect of Exercise	Develops calf and thigh muscles.
Suggestion	The players tug at the soccer ball.

Figure 14–30. Tug of war.

Recovery Time   Three times work rate.

Recovery Exercise   Technique. In pairs, players practice throw-ins for distance.

EXERCISE 20 *The Mule Push*

Number of Players   All players are paired off.

Number of Reps   Three sets each.

Time   Thirty-five seconds.

Method   Two players stand and face the same direction, one behind the other. On command, the back player places the hands on the lower back of the front player and pushes. The front player resists. (See Figure 14–31.)

Effect of Exercise   Develops calf, thigh, and upper body muscles.

Recovery Time   Three times the work rate.

Recovery Exercise   Technique. In pairs, players volley kick and control the ball with the sole of the foot. (See Figure 6–4 page 61.)

Figure 14–31. The mule push.

CHAPTER FIFTEEN

Fun Games

Fun games are a very important part of the soccer training session. Coaches are always searching for new material that will make sessions interesting, rewarding, and self-motivating. Many coaches have found that fun games are the answer. They can turn a frustrated, listless group of players into a highly motivated unit. These games will help players develop qualities such as mobility, strength, power, and team spirit. In addition, the coach's participation in and enthusiasm for some of these games helps convince the players that the coach is human after all.

The games presented in this chapter have been used successfully by many coaches. Fun games are selected and implemented on a rotating basis during the course of the soccer season. These games are suitable for players of all ages.

FUN GAME NUMBER 1 *Chain Tag*

Location	Penalty-area.
Number of Players	All players.
Time	Ten to twelve minutes.
Method	The players gather in the penalty-area or a work area of nearly the same dimensions. The coach selects three of the best athletes, who then join hands. On the coach's command, the three players will try to tag the rest

Figure 15–1. Chain tag.

of the players. All the tagged players join the chain. The last player tagged is declared the winner. (See Figure 15–1.)

Rules	All the players must stay in the penalty-area or work area. Those who leave the designated area are considered tagged.
Effect of Game	It develops the players power off the mark, skill in changing direction, and team work.
Suggestions	1. Every time there is an even number of players on the chain, the players can split up and form another chasing pair.
	2. The game begins with two pairs of players. The pair that tags the most players wins.

FUN GAME NUMBER 2 *Fox and the Hunters*

Location	Penalty-area.
Number of Players	All players (two teams).
Time	Twelve to fifteen minutes.

Figure 15–2. Fox and the hunters.

Method	The players gather in the penalty-area or a work area of approximately the same dimensions. The coach selects two teams to be the hunters. The coach is the fox. On the coach's command, the soccer ball is either dropped or kicked into the work area. The team gaining possession of the ball passes it around basketball style, trying to score a goal by striking the coach. The coach moves and hides among the players within the work area. The opposing team tries to gain ball possession. (See Figure 15–2.)
Rules	To score a goal, the ball must strike the coach on the lower half of the body. Each time a goal is scored, the game is restarted by dropping or kicking a ball into the work area.
Effect of Game	It develops player awareness, teamwork, team spirit, and communication between the players.
Suggestions	1. Select two teams, one made up of forwards, the other made up of backs. Have them play each other.
	2. Introduce another fox into the game.
	3. Play regular soccer.

FUN GAME NUMBER 3 *Spin the Coach or Player*

Location	Anywhere.
Number of Players	Eight to ten players per group.

Figure 15–3. Spin the coach.

Time	Five to eight minutes.
Method	The players are divided into groups of eight to ten players each. Each group sits in a circle. The players extend their legs, so their feet touch in the middle of the circle. The players bring their knees up toward their chests. The coach selects one of the smallest or lightest players to stand in the middle of the circle. The sitting players make the circle tighter and smaller by stretching their arms out toward the standing player's chest. The standing player stiffens up like a board and falls toward the sitting players. They support the falling player's body weight and spin him or her around the circle. (See Figure 15–3.)
Rules	There must not be any space between the sitting players, and their hands and arms must be extended at all times.
Effect of Game	It develops upper body strength in the sitting players. It also develops team spirit and cooperation.
Suggestions	Any sitting player who fails to support the falling player's body weight replaces the falling player.

FUN GAME NUNBER 4 *Walk the Line*

Location	Penalty-area.
Number of Players	All players (two teams).

Figure 15–4. Walk the line.

Time	Ten minutes.
Method	The players gather in the penalty-area. They are divided into two teams. The coach selects two team captains. The captains stand on the goal line, facing the penalty-area perimeter lines. The teams line up at the top of the penalty-area and face their team captains. On the coach's command, the first two players from each team race to the team captain. When they reach the captain, these players put their heads on the captain's midsection. The team captain spins the player around ten times, as fast as possible. The spun player tries to walk or run back along the penalty-area line, rejoin the team, and tag the next player. (See Figure 15–4.)
Rules	All the players on the losing team must do ten push-ups.
Effect of Game	It develops a player's speed off the mark, fosters concentration, and boosts team spirit.
Suggestions	Spun players must walk or run around the center circle.

FUN GAME NUMBER 5 *Regatta*

Location	Goal area.
Number of Players	All players (four teams).

Figure 15–5. Boat race.

Time	Six minutes.
Method	The players gather at the top of the goal area box. The coach selects four teams, each with the same number of players. The first player on each team sits on the goal area line, facing the goal. The rest of the players sit down behind their respective team leaders, lock their legs around the player in front of them, and keep their hands in a ready position. On the coach's command, the teams try to move forward in unison, using only their hands or oars. (See Figure 15–5.)
Rules	Any team, or boat, that starts to come apart must immediately hook back up or be declared "sunk." The first team to get the last person over the goal line will be declared the winner.
Effect of Game	It develops upper body strength, teamwork, and spirit.
Suggestions	a. Give each team a crew name, such as Oxford, Cambridge, Harvard, or Yale.
	b. Encourage the players to chant a rowing ditty.

FUN GAME NUMBER 6 *Submarine*

Location	Goal area.
Number of Players	All players (four teams).

Figure 15–6. Submarine.

Time	Six minutes.
Method	The players gather at the top of the goal area box. The coach selects four teams, each with the same number of players. The first player from each team faces the goal lying on the stomach, arms extended, fingers touching the goal area line. The other players lie down behind their respective team leaders in a similar fashion. Each player grabs the ankles of the player in front of him or her, arms in a bent position. On the coach's command, each team tries to move forward using only elbows and knees. The first players in line may use their hands to pull themselves forward. (See Figure 15–6.)
Rules	Any team or submarine that is breaking apart must immediately join up or be declared "sunk." The first team whose leader touches the goal line with the fingers, team in tow, will be declared the winner.
Effect of Game	It develops player upper body strength, teamwork, and spirit.
Suggestion	Try this on a wet, muddy field.

FUN GAME NUMBER 7 *Crows and Cranes*

Location	Center of the field (half field line).

Figure 15–7. Crows and cranes.

Number of Players	All players (two teams).
Time	Eight to ten minutes.
Method	The players gather at the half field line. The coach selects two teams, crows and cranes. The players sit down across from one another, parallel to the half field line and about four yards apart. The coach calls out a team name—crows, for example. At the same time, the coach points out the direction in which they must run. Players will either run to the safety of their own penalty-area to avoid being tagged by the cranes, or chase the cranes and try to tag them. (See Figure 15–7.)
Rules	The players must try to tag the opposition. Players tagged must rest on one knee. The team that tags the most players after an equal number of runs by both sides is declared the winner.
Effect of Game	It develops player speed off the mark and team spirit.
Suggestions	a. Players lie flat on their backs. b. Players lie flat on their stomachs.

FUN GAME NUMBER 8 *Duck, Duck, Goose*

Location	Center circle.
Number of Players	All players.

Figure 15–8. Duck, duck, goose.

Time	Ten to twelve minutes.
Method	The players gather at the center circle. The coach tells the players to sit about three to four yards apart from one another around the circle. The coach selects one player, the duck, to stand outside of the circle. On the coach's command, this player jogs around the circle, touching the heads of the sitting players and saying "duck, duck." Finally, the duck chooses one of the sitting players to be the goose. The player picks a goose that he or she thinks can be outrun. The duck must run around the circle and back to the sitting player's vacated spot before being tagged by the goose. (See Figure 15–8.)
Rules	The head of every player must be touched. The players must remain seated at all times. Should the goose tag the first player, or duck, the duck will do a given number of push-ups. Every player must be chosen as goose at least once. No player can be chosen as goose more than once.
Effect of Game	It develops player speed off the mark and team spirit.
Suggestion	The players stand in a circle with their legs apart. The duck, after touching the goose, must try to get through a standing player's legs to safety before being tagged by the goose.

FUN GAME NUMBER 9 *Around the Clock*

Location	Center circle.
Number of Players	All players are paired off.

Figure 15–9. Around the clock.

Time	Ten to twelve minutes.
Method	The coach pairs off the players, and then has them stand around the center circle, one behind the other, to form the twelve points of the clock. The pairs are numbered one through twelve. The coach will then call out different times. For example, if the coach calls out "five after two," the players who were given these numbers will sprint around the outside of the circle (clockwise) and return to their original position. (See Figure 15–9.)
Rules	Players must run around the outside of the clock. The last player to return to his or her original position must do push-ups.
Effect of Game	It develops player speed off the mark and team spirit.
Suggestions	a. Instead of racing around the outside of the circle, the players weave around.
	b. The pairs of players run in opposite directions.
	c. When they return to the original spot, the pairs of players mount up, horse and jockey style.

FUN GAME NUMBER 10 *The Numbers Game*

Location   Penalty-area.

Number of   All players.
Players

Time   Four to six minutes.

Method   The coach has the players gather at the top of the penalty-area, facing the half field line. The coach tells the players that the following numbers represent the following actions. One means sprinting forward, two means running backward, three means sitting down, and four means jumping for an imaginary head ball. When the coach calls a number, the players quickly perform the required action.

Rules   If the players' actions differ from those assigned to the given numbers, players will do push-ups.

Effect of   It develops the players' alertness and speed off the mark.
Game

Suggestion   The coach demonstrates an action. The players perform the opposite action and call out the correct number for their action. For example, if the coach runs backward, the players sprint forward and call out the number one.

CHAPTER SIXTEEN

Soccer Equipment

Selecting Shoes

Selecting a pair of soccer shoes takes as much consideration as selecting everyday shoes. Cost, size, suppleness, durability, and type of soles (multi-cleats versus six cleats) must be foremost in the player's mind.

The cost of soccer shoes can vary from as little as ten dollars up to fifty dollars, depending on the player's age and the quality of the soccer shoe selected. Soccer shoes manufactured by American shoe companies cost less than the European shoes, and are of a good quality.

When trying on the soccer shoe for size, the younger player must make allowances for growing feet. Selecting soccer shoes that are a little large will give the player a longer wearing period and help keep cost to a minimum. Buying soccer shoes one half size larger than normal should be sufficient. Wearing two pairs of socks will then give a snug and comfortable fit until the young player grows into the shoes. The older player, whose growth is stabilized, should select soccer shoes that fit the bare foot snugly, and then follow the "break-in" instructions in this chapter.

The soccer shoe's suppleness can be tested by bending and twisting the shoe in all directions. Suppleness is necessary in soccer shoes because of the foot movements made during the course of a soccer game, such as jumping, stopping and starting, and turning quickly. If shoes are too stiff, they can keep the feet from moving naturally and prevent the shoe from hugging the foot, causing the player discomfort.

Durability will depend somewhat on the cost of the shoes. For long-lasting wear, select shoes made from a good grade of cowhide. Look for reinforced toes and heels. Shoes made from cowhide tend to be a little heavier than most imported shoes, which are made from kid and kangaroo. However, they do stand up better and offer protection. Lightweight shoes should be selected only if players are serious about the game and technically competent.

Weaknesses that the player should be aware of occur, in most soccer shoes, along the kicking surfaces in front of and on the outside of the shoe, and where the upper portion of the shoe is welded to the sole. The tongue of the shoe should also be checked, since many of them separate from stitching with constant pulling. Look for shoes that have the tongue built into the upper shoe.

Choose multi-studded cleats instead of six-studded removable cleats only if weather conditions during the course of the soccer season demand them. If the season is dry and the ground is hard, multi-studded cleats should be chosen for better traction and comfort, because the material absorbs the shock of the hard ground. For young players, multi-studded cleats are the only choice at the moment. Since most youngsters play during the late spring and summer, these shoes are a good investment. If the soccer season is wet and fields are soft or muddy, then plastic six-studded removable cleats should be selected. These shoes, because they have more space between the cleats, will give the player better traction and will help prevent slipping and sliding.

Tying Shoes

Tying soccer shoes correctly is very important. Yet, little or no time is spent showing the player the correct way to tie the shoes. Most soccer shoe manufacturers furnish the shoes with laces that are in excess of sixty inches in length. This means that once the shoe has been laced, the player still has to contend with a large length of overhang.

Players often tie this overhanging string into an enormous bow knot across the instep. This is totally unacceptable for the following reasons. First, a large bow knot tied across the top of the instep is in an area where constant contact with the soccer ball is made, especially when volley kicking. This constant playing of the ball on top of a bow knot can help the player develop a bruised instep, which, in turn, can affect the player's performance. Second, a large bow knot can be a safety hazard. It can cause the player's cleats to get caught up in the bow in close tackling situations.

The shoes should be tied in the following way. Lead the laces through the eyelets and through the slot in the tongue to hold the tongue in place. Continue to the top eyelet. Tie an overhand knot, then pass the laces under the shoe and around the arch. Tie another overhand knot and bow on the outside of the shoe, where less contact is made with the ball.

If the soccer shoes have side tabs or lace guides and if the laces are long enough, follow the same tying procedure mentioned above, but do not tie the laces in a bow knot on the outside of the shoe. Rather, after the second overhand knot has been tied, feed the laces through the lace guides on both sides of the shoe and complete with a loose overhand double knot or bow below the heel tab. For easier, quicker shoe tying, no matter what the type of shoes, place the foot on a bench or stool.

Breaking-In and Caring for Shoes

Breaking-in the shoes for play can help to eliminate those pre-season heel and toe blisters that so many players experience. Blisters can affect the player's performance. If shoes are made of leather, then do what the professionals do. Tie the shoes onto the bare feet and soak them in a bucket or under a shower of comfortably warm water for about twenty minutes. Then, take the wet shoes off, dry off the moisture with a soft cloth, stuff them from toe to heel with newspaper, and let them dry. Do not put the shoes close to artificial heat; simply place them in a normally heated room. Fine leather shoes must never be put near a radiator or other heat, since the natural moisture and oils in the leather will disappear and the leather will become stiff and dry and will crack. After the shoes are thoroughly dry, in about twenty-four to thirty-six hours, apply a good leather preservative both inside and out.

Shoes should be cleaned after every wearing. A stiff brush will take off most of the mud, grass, and dirt. A small blunt stick will remove caked-on dirt between the cleats and the upper shoe area. After every few days of wear, apply a light coating of a leather preservative to replace the oils that hard wear and dust remove. After playing on a wet field, or in the rain, clean and dry the shoes as soon as possible. Stuff the shoes with newspaper and let them dry. Always oil the shoes after they have dried.

SOCCER BALLS

Soccer balls can be purchased in three different sizes: size three for ages seven to nine, size four for ages ten to twelve, and full size, number five, for ages thirteen and up. Prices range from twelve to sixty dollars, depending on the ball's size and quality. The life of the ball will vary according to its quality and how well it is taken care of. Soccer balls that are manufactured from leather or poromeric are the most popular. They are a good value for the money.

Whether the soccer ball will last for any period of time will depend largely on whether or not the player follows the recommended air pressure guidelines shown on the ball's casing. Following is a quick method for checking the ball for correct air pressure when no air gauge is available.

Using your full body weight, press your thumbs onto the casing of the ball. If the thumbs make no indentation whatsoever, the ball is over-inflated. If the thumbs make an indentation very easily, the ball is too soft. If the thumbs make a slight indentation, the ball has approximately the proper air pressure for game play.

Immediately after game play or a practice session, the soccer ball should be deflated before it is put into storage. This will prevent a weakness from occurring in the inner tube because of temperature changes. Such a weakness can cause the soccer ball to lose its shape or lose air. Also, players should be discouraged from sitting on the soccer ball, since this also causes the soccer ball to lose its shape. The player's body weight compresses the air in the ball, puts stress on the inner tube, and forces it to stretch, weaken, and bulge.

Glossary of Soccer Terms

Balance in Defense: Defending players remain or move into predetermined positions or areas of the field. They refuse to be drawn out of position by movement of opponents, or the ball.

The Ball Control: To kill the ball so that it drops or stops at the feet.

Banana Shot: The ball curves while it is in the air or along the ground, after it has been kicked with the instep or the outside of the foot. The foot strikes the ball to the right or left side of the center, depending on the situation presented the kicker.

Center Back: Responsible for stopping attacks through the center of the field and the penalty-area. Makes tackles and interceptions.

Chest Trap: To kill an air ball with the chest so that it drops to the feet.

Chip: To loft the ball over both short and long distances by striking the ball sharply at the lowest point possible.

Cover: To protect players or space when defending.

Cushion: To absorb the impact of a ground or air ball pass by withdrawing the controlling surface just as the ball strikes it.

Delay in Defense: To contain and slow down the ball carrier, thereby allowing supporting defending players to take up covering positions.

Depth in Attack: Supporting attacking players moving into positions to receive the ball, regardless of location and distance from the ball carrier. This offers a full range of passing opportunities.

Depth in Defense: All around support by defending players for the defender challenging for ball.

Dribble: To use a series of pushes or taps with the feet while moving to keep the ball under control.

Feint: A deceptive movement by a player to confuse an opponent.

Head: Any shot hit with the head.

Head Flick: To glance or touch the ball with the head so as to redirect an air ball's flight.

Head Shot: Heading with power and direction into the opponent's goal.

Instep: The large bone starting at the base of the large toe and extending up and back to the ankle. Soccer shoelaces are laced along the instep.

Instep Kick: To shoot or pass a ground ball with the instep.

Instep Volley Kick: To shoot or pass an air ball with the instep.

Inswinger: An air ball that curves in toward the goal.

Lateral Mobility: The ability to move side to side.

Lead Pass: To pass the ball forward to an intended receiver at a speed that coincides with the speed of the receiver.

Mark: To stand close to the opponent.

Mobility in Attack: Movement on and off the ball by attacking players in an effort to draw defending players out of position.

Midfielders: The "link" between the defensive and offensive line, often referred to as the playmakers.

Penetration in Attack: To dribble or pass the ball rapidly through the opposing team's defense.

Pressure of an Opponent: Tight marking. Closing down the attacking players' time and space.

Scissor or Bicycle Kick: To kick the ball over the head while it is in mid-air.

Screening: To place the body between an opponent and the soccer ball.

Slide Tackle: To slide or push the ball away from the ball carrier's feet.

Square Pass: One of a series of passes across the field to supporting players who are in a straight line.

Strikers: Central offensive line players responsible for scoring the bulk of the team's goals.

Sweeper: The last defensive player who can intercept passes or runs before they reach the goalkeeper.

Thigh Trap: To kill an air ball with the thigh so that it drops to the feet.

Toe Trap: To kill an air ball with the front of the foot. The foot is raised approximately one inch off the surface to meet the ball and then lowered.

Wall Pass: A pass that has a rebound effect. The ball is passed to a supporting player and immediately returned to the passer.

Wingers: Players on the offensive line who play close to the touchline. Usually very fast and clever dribblers of the ball.

Wing Fullbacks: Defensive players responsible for challenging the opposing winger for the ball.

Index